DATE DUE

Return Material Promptly

Hate Crimes

Hate Crimes

David L. Hudson Jr.

SERIES CONSULTING EDITOR
Alan Marzilli, M.A., J.D.

CHELSEA HOUSE
PUBLISHERS
An imprint of Infobase Publishing

Hate Crimes

Chelsea House
An imprint of Infobase Publishing
132 West 31st Street
New York NY 10001

Library of Congress Cataloging-in-Publication Data

Hudson, David L., 1969–
  Hate crimes / by David L. Hudson.
    p. cm. — (Point/Counterpoint)
  Includes bibliographical references and index.
  ISBN 978-1-60413-437-7 (hardcover)
  1. Hate crimes—United States. I. Title. II. Series.
  KF9345.H83 2009
  345.73'025—dc22   2008049449

Chelsea House books are available at special discounts when purchased in bulk quantities for businesses, associations, institutions, or sales promotions. Please call our Special Sales Department in New York at (212) 967-8800 or (800) 322-8755.

You can find Chelsea House on the World Wide Web at
http://www.chelseahouse.com

Series design by Keith Trego
Cover design by Keith Trego and Alicia Post

Printed in the United States of America

Bang NMSG 10 9 8 7 6 5 4 3 2 1

This book is printed on acid-free paper.

All links and Web addresses were checked and verified to be correct at the time of publication. Because of the dynamic nature of the Web, some addresses and links may have changed since publication and may no longer be valid.

FOREWORD ||||▷

Alan Marzilli, M.A., J.D.
Birmingham, Alabama

The POINT/COUNTERPOINT series offers the reader a greater understanding of some of the most controversial issues in contemporary American society—issues such as capital punishment, immigration, gay rights, and gun control. We have looked for the most contemporary issues and have included topics—such as the controversies surrounding "blogging"—that we could not have imagined when the series began.

In each volume, the author has selected an issue of particular importance and set out some of the key arguments on both sides of the issue. Why study both sides of the debate? Maybe you have yet to make up your mind on an issue, and the arguments presented in the book will help you to form an opinion. More likely, however, you will already have an opinion on many of the issues covered by the series. There is always the chance that you will change your opinion after reading the arguments for the other side. But even if you are firmly committed to an issue—for example, school prayer or animal rights—reading both sides of the argument will help you to become a more effective advocate for your cause. By gaining an understanding of opposing arguments, you can develop answers to those arguments.

Perhaps more importantly, listening to the other side sometimes helps you see your opponent's arguments in a more human way. For example, Sister Helen Prejean, one of the nation's most visible opponents of capital punishment, has been deeply affected by her interactions with the families of murder victims. By seeing the families' grief and pain, she understands much better why people support the death penalty, and she is able to carry out her advocacy with a greater sensitivity to the needs and beliefs of death penalty supporters.

The books in the series include numerous features that help the reader to gain a greater understanding of the issues. Real-life examples illustrate the human side of the issues. Each chapter also includes excerpts from relevant laws, court cases, and other material, which provide a better foundation for understanding the arguments. The volumes contain citations to relevant sources of law and information, and an appendix guides the reader through the basics of legal research, both on the Internet and in the library. Today, through free Web sites, it is easy to access legal documents, and these books might give you ideas for your own research.

Studying the issues covered by the POINT/COUNTERPOINT series is more than an academic activity. The issues described in the books affect all of us as citizens. They are the issues that today's leaders debate and tomorrow's leaders will decide. While all of the issues covered in the POINT/COUNTERPOINT series are controversial today, and will remain so for the foreseeable future, it is entirely possible that the reader might one day play a central role in resolving the debate. Today it might seem that some debates—such as capital punishment and abortion—will never be resolved.

However, our nation's history is full of debates that seemed as though they never would be resolved, and many of the issues are now well settled—at least on the surface. In the nineteenth century, abolitionists met with widespread resistance to their efforts to end slavery. Ultimately, the controversy threatened the union, leading to the Civil War between the northern and southern states. Today, while a public debate over the merits of slavery would be unthinkable, racism persists in many aspects of society.

Similarly, today nobody questions women's right to vote. Yet at the beginning of the twentieth century, suffragists fought public battles for women's voting rights, and it was not until the passage of the Nineteenth Amendment in 1920 that the legal right of women to vote was established nationwide.

What makes an issue controversial? Often, controversies arise when most people agree that there is a problem, but people disagree about the best way to solve the problem. There is little argument that poverty is a major problem in the United States, especially in inner cities and rural areas. Yet, people disagree vehemently about the best way to address the problem. To some, the answer is social programs, such as welfare, food stamps, and public housing. However, many argue that such subsidies encourage dependence on government benefits while unfairly penalizing those who work and pay taxes, and that the real solution is to require people to support themselves.

American society is in a constant state of change, and sometimes modern practices clash with what many consider to be "traditional values," which are often rooted in conservative political views or religious beliefs. Many blame high crime rates, and problems such as poverty, illiteracy, and drug use on the breakdown of the traditional family structure of a married mother and father raising their children. Since the "sexual revolution" of the 1960s and 1970s, sparked in part by the widespread availability of the birth control pill, marriage rates have declined, and the number of children born outside of marriage has increased. The sexual revolution led to controversies over birth control, sex education, and other issues, most prominently abortion. Similarly, the gay rights movement has been challenged as a threat to traditional values. While many gay men and lesbians want to have the same right to marry and raise families as heterosexuals, many politicians and others have challenged gay marriage and adoption as a threat to American society.

Sometimes, new technology raises issues that we have never faced before, and society disagrees about the best solution. Are people free to swap music online, or does this violate the copyright laws that protect songwriters and musicians' ownership of the music that they create? Should scientists use "genetic engineering" to create new crops that are resistant to disease and pests and produce more food, or is it too risky to use a laboratory to create plants that nature never intended? Modern medicine has continued to increase the average lifespan—which is now 77 years, up from under 50 years at the beginning of the twentieth century—but many people are now choosing to die in comfort rather than living with painful ailments in their later years. For doctors, this presents an ethical dilemma: should they allow their patients to die? Should they assist patients in ending their own lives painlessly?

Perhaps the most controversial issues are those that implicate a Constitutional right. The Bill of Rights—the first 10 Amendments to the U.S. Constitution—spell out some of the most fundamental rights that distinguish our democracy from other nations with fewer freedoms. However, the sparsely worded document is open to interpretation, with each side saying that the Constitution is on their side. The Bill of Rights was meant to protect individual liberties; however, the needs of some individuals clash with society's needs. Thus, the Constitution often serves as a battleground between individuals and government officials seeking to protect society in some way. The First Amendment's guarantee of "freedom of speech" leads to some very difficult questions. Some forms of expression—such as burning an American flag—lead to public outrage, but are protected by the First Amendment. Other types of expression that most people find objectionable—such as child pornography—are not protected by the Constitution. The question is not only where to draw the line, but whether drawing lines around constitutional rights threatens our liberty.

The Bill of Rights raises many other questions about individual rights and societal "good." Is a prayer before a high school football game an "establishment of religion" prohibited by the First Amendment? Does the Second Amendment's promise of "the right to bear arms" include concealed handguns? Does stopping and frisking someone standing on a known drug corner constitute "unreasonable search and seizure" in violation of the Fourth Amendment? Although the U.S. Supreme Court has the ultimate authority in interpreting the U.S. Constitution, their answers do not always satisfy the public. When a group of nine people—sometimes by a five-to-four vote—makes a decision that affects hundreds of millions of others, public outcry can be expected. For example, the Supreme Court's 1973 ruling in *Roe v. Wade* that abortion is protected by the Constitution did little to quell the debate over abortion.

Whatever the root of the controversy, the books in the POINT/ COUNTERPOINT series seek to explain to the reader the origins of the debate, the current state of the law, and the arguments on either side of the debate. Our hope in creating this series is that the reader will be better informed about the issues facing not only our politicians, but all of our nation's citizens, and become more actively involved in resolving these debates, as voters, concerned citizens, journalists, or maybe even elected officials.

This volume examines the regulation of crimes that were motivated by hatred against specific groups of people. Although American society has made a great deal of progress in combating racism, sexism, and other forms of discrimination, prejudice against certain groups persists. Driven to the fringes of society, hate often boils over into violence—against racial and ethnic minorities, immigrants, gays, lesbians, and transgender people, and members of religious groups.

Some crimes—such as murder, assault, and vandalism—are punishable by law regardless of motive. However, the question of whether to punish these crimes more severely when prejudice is the motive remains controversial. When a crime is committed against someone because of his or her sexual orientation or gender identity, the controversy is even greater. A related debate is whether to punish overt symbols of hatred, in particular the displaying of a hangman's noose, when the motive is discriminatory. In this volume, the reader will explore both sides of these issues and have the opportunity to weigh the balance between protecting public safety and upholding constitutional rights.

What Are Hate Crimes? An Overview of Their Development

Nearly 1 year ago . . . I was viciously attacked by two individuals because of my heritage as a Mexican-American. . . . After I was sucker-punched and knocked out, I was dragged into the back-yard for an attack that would last for over an hour. Two indi-viduals, one an admitted racist skinhead, attempted to carve a swastika on my chest. After they stripped me naked, they burned me with a cigarette, and I was kicked by the skinhead's steel-toed army boots. . . . Reportedly, I lay unconscious in the backyard of the private residence for the next 8 to 9 hours.

Testimony of David Ritcheson, hate-crime victim,
before the U.S. House of Representatives in 2007.[1]

Hate crimes occur when individuals purposely select their victims and inflict violence or other intimidating acts upon those victims because of specific characteristics, such as race, religion, national origin, or gender. A recent report filed before members of a U.S. House of Representatives committee explained the danger and harm of hate crimes: "They materially and unacceptably interfere with the full participation of all Americans in the fundamental liberties enjoyed in our democratic society."[2]

A Brief History of Hate Crimes

Hate crimes have occurred throughout history. Hatred, bigotry, racial prejudice, and religious differences have led to innumerable conflicts, bloodshed, and even world wars. The U.S. Justice Department's Bureau of Justice Statistics states that "the problem of hate crimes is hardly a recent phenomenon. . . . [H]ate crimes have shaped and sometimes defined the history of nations."[3] "Ethnic cleansings" have occurred and unfortunately still occur in certain places around the globe. The Holocaust—in which an estimated 6 million European Jews were systematically exterminated under the orders of German leader Adolf Hitler—was an example of a monstrous hate crime.[4] In U.S. history, the shackling of slaves and the forced relocation of Native Americans to reservations could be classified as hate crimes. For nearly a century, the Ku Klux Klan, an organization of white racists, often lynched individuals because of their race and terrorized African Americans who attempted to vote and change the legal system.

In the wake of the civil-rights movement in the 1960s, Congress passed a civil-rights law that is seen as a precursor to modern hate-crime laws. This federal law outlines criminal penalties for anyone who "by force or threat of force willfully injures, intimidates or interferes with, or attempts to injure, intimidate or interfere with" a series of federally protected rights, such as voting and serving on a jury.[5] This law, however, applies only in specific circumstances when a victim is attempting to exercise one of six listed "federally protected rights." It left many people believing that the federal government needed to do more to combat hate crimes.

Pictured, Ku Klux Klan Grand Wizard Thom Robb (*center, wearing glasses*) leading fellow robed and hooded Klan members in a white power salute in front of a burning cross at a KKK rally. In its various incarnations, the Ku Klux Klan, an organization of white racists, has terrorized and lynched African Americans and other minorities.

In the 1980s and 1990s, hate crime legislation appeared at an accelerated pace across the United States to address a perceived problem of bias-motivated crimes. Certain events raised the public's consciousness regarding hate crimes. For example, an infamous beating of three African Americans in the predominately white New York City neighborhood of Howard Beach touched off a nationwide debate on the problem of race-based hate in the mid–1980s.[6] In 1983, the U.S. Commission on Civil

THE LETTER OF THE LAW

Hate Crime Statistics Act of 1990

28 U.S. Code § 535, n.

(b)(1) Under the authority of section 534 of title 28, United States Code, the Attorney General shall acquire data, for the calendar year 1990 and each of the succeeding 4 calendar years, about crimes that manifest evidence of prejudice based on race, religion, sexual orientation, or ethnicity, including where appropriate the crimes of murder, non-negligent manslaughter; forcible rape; aggravated assault, simple assault, intimidation; arson; and destruction, damage or vandalism of property.

(2) The Attorney General shall establish guidelines for the collection of such data including the necessary evidence and criteria that must be present for a finding of manifest prejudice and procedures for carrying out the purposes of this section.

(3) Nothing in this section creates a cause of action or a right to bring an action, including an action based on discrimination due to sexual orientation. As used in this section, the term "sexual orientation" means consensual homosexuality or heterosexuality. This subsection does not limit any existing cause of action or right to bring an action, including any action under the Administrative Procedure Act or the All Writs Act.

(4) Data acquired under this section shall be used only for research or statistical purposes and may not contain any information that may reveal the identity of an individual victim of a crime.

(5) The Attorney General shall publish an annual summary of the data acquired under this section.

Rights recommended that the federal government investigate bias-motivated crimes. Two years later, Congress held its first hearing on hate crimes. The term "hate crime" entered the public consciousness on a larger scale that year when several Democratic members of Congress—John Conyers of Michigan, Barbara Kennedy of Connecticut, and Mario Biaggi of New York—introduced a bill called the Hate Crime Statistics Act.[7] After considerable debate, it was passed in 1990. The Hate Crime Statistics Act requires the federal government to collect statistics on hate crimes involving race, religion, national origin, and sexual orientation; the Federal Bureau of Investigation (FBI) is responsible for publishing an annual hate-crimes statistics report. Several states, including Maryland and Pennsylvania, had passed similar measures. Congress amended the Hate Crime Statistics

THE LETTER OF THE LAW

Hate-Crime Provisions of the Violent Crime Control and Law Enforcement Act

28 U.S. Code 994.

(a) DEFINITION—In this section, "hate crime" means a crime in which the defendant intentionally selects a victim, or in the case of a property crime, the property that is the object of the crime, because of the actual or perceived race, color, religion, national origin, ethnicity, gender, disability, or sexual orientation of any person.

(b) SENTENCING ENHANCEMENT—Pursuant to section 994 of title 28, United States Code, the United States Sentencing Commission shall promulgate guidelines or amend existing guidelines to provide sentencing enhancements of not less than 3 offense levels for offenses that the finder of fact at trial determines beyond a reasonable doubt are hate crimes. In carrying out this section, the United States Sentencing Commission shall ensure that there is reasonable consistency with other guidelines, avoid duplicative punishments for substantially the same offense, and take into account any mitigating circumstances that might justify exceptions.

Act to require the FBI to include statistics of hate crimes committed against the disabled. Then, in 1996, Congress made the Hate Crime Statistics Act a permanent law.

In 1994, Congress passed the Violent Crime Control and Law Enforcement Act. This law required longer prison sentences for persons who commit hate crimes on federal land because of a victim's "race, color, national origin, ethnicity, gender, disability or sexual orientation." The "federal land" limitation requirement, however, had proponents of strong hate-crimes hoping for more widespread federal regulation.

In 1995, a series of church burnings occurred across the southern United States. Congress quickly passed the Church Arson Prevention Act of 1996. This law increased penalties for damaging churches and other religious property.[8] Hate crimes entered the public consciousness again in 1998, largely as a result of two murders. The first, committed in June, involved several white men beating and dragging James Byrd, a black man, to his death behind their truck. The second occurred in October when a young gay man named Matthew Shepard was beaten, burned, chained to a fence, and left to die in freezing temperatures. These two crimes, committed because of racial and anti-gay prejudice, fueled the push for greater federal involvement in hate crimes.

Most hate-crime legislation has been passed in the states. There are different types of hate-crime statutes. Many hate-crime statutes are referred to as ethnic-intimidation or civil-rights-intimidation statutes. These laws provide a criminal penalty for harassing someone based on certain characteristics.

Another type of hate-crime law is often referred to as a penalty-enhancement law because it allows a defendant's criminal sentence for an underlying crime, such as assault or battery, to be increased if the defendant intentionally selected his victim because of discriminatory bias. For example, Vermont has a law for "hate-motivated crimes" that allows a criminal's sentence for

THE LETTER OF THE LAW

Tennessee's Civil-Rights Intimidation Law

39–17–309. Civil rights intimidation.

(a) The general assembly finds and declares that it is the right of every person regardless of race, color, ancestry, religion or national origin, to be secure and protected from fear, intimidation, harassment and bodily injury caused by the activities of groups and individuals. It is not the intent of this section to interfere with the exercise of rights protected by the constitution of the United States. The general assembly recognizes the constitutional right of every citizen to harbor and express beliefs on any subject whatsoever and to associate with others who share similar beliefs. The general assembly further finds that the advocacy of unlawful acts by groups or individuals against other persons or groups for the purpose of inciting and provoking damage to property and bodily injury or death to persons is not constitutionally protected, poses a threat to public order and safety, and should be subject to criminal sanctions.

(b) A person commits the offense of intimidating others from exercising civil rights who:

    (1) Injures or threatens to injure or coerces another person with the intent to unlawfully intimidate another from the free exercise or enjoyment of any right or privilege secured by the constitution or laws of the state of Tennessee;

    (2) Injures or threatens to injure or coerces another person with the intent to unlawfully intimidate another because that other exercised any right or privilege secured by the constitution or laws of the United States or the constitution or laws of the state of Tennessee;

    (3) Damages, destroys or defaces any real or personal property of another person with the intent to unlawfully intimidate another from the free exercise or enjoyment of any right or privilege secured by the constitution or laws of the state of Tennessee; or

    (4) Damages, destroys or defaces any real or personal property of another person with the intent to unlawfully intimidate another because that other exercised any right or privilege secured by the constitution or laws of the United States or the constitution or laws of the state of Tennessee.

(continues)

(continued)
   (c) It is an offense for a person to wear a mask or disguise with the intent to violate subsection (b).
   (d) A violation of subsection (b) is a Class D felony. A violation of subsection (c) is a Class A misdemeanor.
   (e) The penalties provided in this section for intimidating others from exercising civil rights do not preclude victims from seeking any other remedies, criminal or civil, otherwise available under law.

lower-range offenses to be enhanced if the person is "maliciously motivated by the victim's actual or perceived race, color, religion, national origin, sex, ancestry, age, service in the armed forces of the United States, handicap, sexual orientation or gender identity."[9]

Controversy

Hate-crimes laws continue to be controversial. Proponents insist that such laws are necessary because hate crimes cause greater harm than other crimes. New York City Mayor Edward Koch wrote in 1987:

> Why is this legislation important? Because hate crimes are different from other crimes, they require a different governmental response. Unlike other criminal behavior, hate crimes are motivated by prejudice against an entire group of people, based on their color, religion, ethnicity, national origin, gender or sexual preference. For this reason, hate crimes, if not responded to, tend to undermine the tolerance necessary in our pluralistic society.[10]

Similarly, Representative Sheila Jackson Lee, D-Texas, noted that "it is not the frequency of these crimes alone that distinguish these acts of violence from other types of crime; it is the impact these crimes have on the victims, their families, their communities and, in some instances, the nation."[11]

Opponents of such legislation, however, insist that hate-crime laws are unconstitutional, unnecessary, and do more harm than good. They contend that a crime is a crime whether done because a person is bigoted or simply greedy or desperate. For example, murder is murder. Timothy Lynch contends, "it is not necessary or desirable for a hierarchy of hatred to be written into our criminal code."[12] Others suggest that hate-crime laws violate the equal-protection clause of the Constitution because they treat victims of crime and crimes themselves differently. Nat Hentoff, a critic of such laws, writes: "So much for 'equal protection of the laws.' "[13]

THE LETTER OF THE LAW

Penalty Enhancement Provision in Vermont

§ 1455. Hate-motivated crimes

A person who commits, causes to be committed or attempts to commit any crime and whose conduct is maliciously motivated by the victim's actual or perceived race, color, religion, national origin, sex, ancestry, age, service in the armed forces of the United States, handicap as defined by 21 V.S.A. § 495d(5), sexual orientation or gender identity shall be subject to the following penalties:

(1) If the maximum penalty for the underlying crime is one year or less, the penalty for a violation of this section shall be imprisonment for not more than two years or a fine of not more than $2,000.00, or both.

(2) If the maximum penalty for the underlying crime is more than one year but less than five years, the penalty for a violation of this section shall be imprisonment for not more than five years or a fine of not more than $10,000.00, or both.

(3) If the maximum penalty for the underlying crime is five years or more, the penalty for the underlying crime shall apply; however, the court shall consider the motivation of the defendant as a factor in sentencing.

This book examines three contentious issues involving hate-crime legislation. The first deals with the specific example of the aforementioned penalty enhancement laws. This particular brand of hate-crime laws causes the most controversy because it treats the same crimes—assault or murder, for example—differently based on the bigoted thoughts of the perpetrators. Supporters argue that such laws are necessary to send a strong societal message that hate crimes will not be tolerated and to emphasize the unique dangers that hate crimes cause. Opponents counter that hate-crime laws violate equal protection, freedom of speech, and other constitutional rights.

The second deals with whether states should pass laws criminalizing the display of nooses as a hate crime. Supporters point out that the hangman's noose, like the burning cross, is an especially jarring symbol of racism and segregation. Opponents counter that criminalizing symbols violates First Amendment freedoms and has no logical ending point.

The third and final issue examined in this book concerns whether federal hate-crimes laws should be extended to cover people who are discriminated against because of their sexual orientation. Supporters point out that crimes against gays and lesbians remain a huge problem in society. They emphasize that without legislation against it, gay-bashing will remain an all-too-frequent occurrence. Supporters also argue that the resources of the federal government can make a positive difference in battling such crimes. Opponents counter that many state laws do cover sexual orientation and that extending federal law can lead to the prosecution of those who express their opposition to homosexuality because of their religious beliefs. They also argue that gays and lesbians do not deserve special treatment under the law and that such an expansion of federal authority may infringe on local and state autonomy and exceed the enumerated, or listed, powers of Congress.

Penalty-Enhancement Laws for Hate Crimes Are Constitutional, Effective, and Necessary to Combat and Deter Hate Crimes

I n 1988, Todd Mitchell, a young African-American man, emerged from the movie *Mississippi Burning* feeling enraged at the senseless injustices perpetrated against members of his race. The award-winning film, which features noted actors such as Gene Hackman and Willem Dafoe, portrays the brutal killing of three civil-rights workers by white racists in Mississippi in 1964.

After the movie, Mitchell told a group of his friends, "Do you all feel hyped up to move on some white people?"[1] When Mitchell saw 14-year-old Gregory Riddick, he allegedly yelled: "There goes a white boy; go get him."[2] He and his friends then chased down Riddick and beat him senseless. Riddick was in a coma for four days. A reviewing court determined that if Riddick had not received medical treatment, his injuries could have been fatal.

Such a senseless crime, based upon the victim's race, should be punished severely. Society has a right to send the strongest message possible that such hate crimes will not be tolerated. One common response has been to do what the prosecutors in Kenosha, Wisconsin, did in the Todd Mitchell case: They sought to enhance his sentence based upon the fact that it was also a violent hate crime.

A penalty enhancement law enables prosecutors to charge a perpetrator with a more severe sentence if perpetrators intentionally select their victims based on race, religion, color, disability, or other characteristics. These laws not only punish dangerous hate mongers for a longer period of time, but they also send a message to the community that hate crimes will not be tolerated.

Bias-motivated crimes are more harmful.

Penalty-enhancement laws are necessary to combat the type of crime that may not occur at all but for a person's race, religion, sexual orientation, gender, disability, or other characteristic. These crimes are often significantly more violent and cause much greater harm on the community when committed.[3] Bias-motivated crimes result in the hospitalization of victims at a rate of more than four times the rates of other crimes.[4] Nearly

THE LETTER OF THE LAW

Freedom of speech is protected by the First Amendment to the U.S. Constitution. The First Amendment is the first 45 words of the Bill of Rights:

Congress shall make no law respecting an establishment of religion or the free exercise thereof, or abridging the freedom of speech, or of the press or the right of the people peaceably to assemble and to petition the government for a redress of grievances.

three-quarters of these hate crimes involved assaults with a deadly weapon.

"The potential impact on society of bias-motivated crimes at large is grave," wrote the Anti-Defamation League, which monitors hate crimes. "These crimes tear at the fragile bonds that hold together America's diverse and pluralistic society. They heighten tension, anxiety and feelings of hopelessness in entire communities."[5] Hate-crime victims suffer symptoms of depression and post-traumatic stress disorder more than other crime victims.[6] These crimes "have a unique capacity to terrorize entire groups, to interfere with constitutionally protected activity, and to trigger retaliatory criminal acts."[7]

Bias-motivated crimes deserve greater punishment because they can terrify an entire community more readily than other crimes. "The impact of bias-motivated crimes on the larger community is grave," wrote the Anti-Defamation League in its brief in *Wisconsin v. Mitchell*. "These crimes not only heighten the general feeling of vulnerability, but also directly intimidate the entire segment of the community with which the victim is identified, making large sections of the population feel unprotected by the law."[8]

Victims ordinarily can do nothing to appease their attackers if they are attacked because of their race, sex, or religion. As the California Association of Human Rights Organizations noted, "the violent purpose behind the crime generally eliminates the opportunity for a victim to lessen his or her injury through any meaningful act of compliance."[9] Bias-motivated crimes also are more likely to involve multiple offenders, increasing the likelihood of greater harm to victims. Many highly publicized hate crimes involved attacks by groups upon single individuals.[10]

Penalty enhancement statutes do not violate the First Amendment.

Penalty enhancement statutes do not violate the free-speech rights of criminal defendants. Rather, they are a valid, legislative response to crimes committed by very troubling offenders. No less an authority than the U.S. Supreme Court approved of a penalty enhancement statute in the Todd Mitchell case. In upholding the statute, Chief Justice William H. Rehnquist, writing for a unanimous court, explained, "the Wisconsin statute singles out for enhancement bias-inspired conduct because this conduct is thought to inflict greater individual and societal harm."[11]

Mitchell's defense team argued that the enhanced sentence in his case essentially amounted to thought control because it punished Mitchell for his bigoted thoughts. The Supreme Court, however, explained that Mitchell was not punished for his abstract thoughts, but for his actions. Hate speech may be protected under the law—unless it crosses the line into certain unprotected categories such as "fighting words," true threats, or incitement to imminent lawless action. If Todd Mitchell simply had yelled a racial slur, such speech, while deplorable, likely would not have resulted in criminal punishment. Mitchell, however, did more than simply yell. He and others beat the young

FROM THE BENCH

Wisconsin v. Mitchell, 508 U.S. 476, 487–489 (1993)

According to the State and its amici, bias-motivated crimes are more likely to provoke retaliatory crimes, inflict distinct emotional harms on their victims, and incite community unrest. The State's desire to redress these perceived harms provides an adequate explanation for its penalty-enhancement provision over and above mere disagreement with offenders' beliefs or biases....

The First Amendment, moreover, does not prohibit the evidentiary use of speech to establish the elements of a crime or to prove motive or intent. Evidence of a defendant's previous declarations or statements is commonly admitted in criminal trials subject to evidentiary rules dealing with relevancy, reliability, and the like.

man severely *because of* his race. This is the essence of a hate crime that is punishable by a stiffer penalty.

Numerous other federal and state courts have rejected First Amendment challenges to hate-crime laws that provide for enhanced penalties. In *State v. McKnight*, the Iowa Supreme Court rejected the constitutional challenges of Keith McKnight, a white man who uttered numerous racial slurs to Jonathan Rone, an African-American motorist, and then beat him. McKnight contended that Iowa's hate-crime law violated his First Amendment rights and was too broad. The Iowa Supreme Court, relying on the U.S. Supreme Court's decision in *Wisconsin v. Mitchell*, rejected McKnight's First Amendment-based challenges. Talking about both the Wisconsin law evaluated by the U.S. Supreme Court and its own state law, the Iowa Supreme Court wrote: "In each instance, the legislatures had good reason for the enhancement provisions."[12]

Penalty enhancement laws can deter future hate crimes.

Penalty-enhancement laws for hate crimes help to deter people from committing such heinous crimes. In an amicus brief before the U.S. Supreme Court, the Anti-Defamation League and other groups wrote how "law enforcement officials believe these laws can have a deterrent effect by making clear that hate crimes will be considered particularly serious crimes and will be dealt with accordingly. While there have been no empirical studies on the point, law enforcement officials have recognized the potential deterrent effect of hate crime laws."[13]

Enhanced penalties for hate crimes will not deter every person who may consider committing a hate crime. Such penalties, however, will have a deterrent effect on many of them. Laurie Levin and Michael Sheetz of the Anti-Defamation League explain: "Indeed, among the most outspoken supporters of hate

(continues on page 28)

THE LETTER OF THE LAW

Selected Penalty Enhancement Hate-Crime Laws

Delaware Criminal Code § 1304.

(a) Any person who commits, or attempts to commit, any crime as defined by the laws of this State, and who intentionally:

(1) Commits said crime for the purpose of interfering with the victim's free exercise or enjoyment of any right, privilege or immunity protected by the First Amendment to the United States Constitution, or commits said crime because the victim has exercised or enjoyed said rights; or

(2) Selects the victim because of the victim's race, religion, color, disability, sexual orientation, national origin or ancestry, shall be guilty of a hate crime. For purposes of this section, the term "sexual orientation" means heterosexuality, bisexuality, or homosexuality.

(b) Hate crimes shall be punished as follows:

(1) If the underlying offense is a violation or unclassified misdemeanor, the hate crime shall be a class A misdemeanor;

(2) If the underlying offense is a class A, B, or C misdemeanor, the hate crime shall be a class G felony;

(3) If the underlying offense is a class C, D, E, F, or G felony, the hate crime shall be one grade higher than the underlying offense;

(4) If the underlying offense is a class A or B felony, the hate crime shall be the same grade as the underlying offense, and the minimum sentence of imprisonment required for the underlying offense shall be doubled.

Mississippi Code Ann. 99-19-307. Amount penalty may be enhanced.

In the event it is found beyond a reasonable doubt that the offense was committed by reason of the actual or perceived race, color, ancestry, ethnicity, religion, national origin or gender of the victim, then the penalty for the offense may be enhanced by punishment for a term of imprisonment of up to twice that authorized by law for the offense committed, or a fine of up to twice that authorized by law for the offense committed, or both.

Montana Code Ann. 45-5-222

(1) A person who has pleaded guilty or nolo contendere to or who has been found guilty of any offense, except malicious intimidation or harassment,

that was committed because of the victim's race, creed, religion, color, national origin, or involvement in civil rights or human rights activities or that involved damage, destruction, or attempted destruction of a building regularly used for religious worship, in addition to the punishment provided for commission of the offense, may, if the provisions of 46-1-401 have been complied with, be sentenced to a term of imprisonment of not less than 2 years or more than 10 years.

New Hampshire Sect. 651:6 Extended Term of Imprisonment.

I. A convicted person may be sentenced according to paragraph III if the jury also finds beyond a reasonable doubt that such person:

(a) Based on the circumstances for which he or she is to be sentenced, has knowingly devoted himself or herself to criminal activity as a major source of livelihood;

(b) Has been subjected to a court-ordered psychiatric examination on the basis of which the jury finds that such person is a serious danger to others due to a gravely abnormal mental condition;

(c) Has manifested exceptional cruelty or depravity in inflicting death or serious bodily injury on the victim of the crime;

(d) Has committed an offense involving the use of force against a person with the intention of taking advantage of the victim's age or physical disability;

(e) Has committed or attempted to commit any of the crimes defined in RSA 631 or 632-A against a person under 13 years of age;

(f) Was substantially motivated to commit the crime because of hostility towards the victim's religion, race, creed, sexual orientation as defined in RSA 21:49, national origin or sex;

Nevada Rev. Stat. Ann. 193.1675

[A]ny person who willfully violates ... because the actual or perceived race, color, religion, national origin, physical or mental disability or sexual orientation of the victim was different from that characteristic of the perpetrator may, in addition to the term of imprisonment prescribed by statute for the crime, be punished by imprisonment in the state prison for a minimum term of not less than 1 year and a maximum term of not more than 20 years.

(continued from page 25)
crime initiatives have been police chiefs, sheriffs and prosecutors. Hate crime laws have achieved widespread support in this
country because they address a fundamental societal problem
and do so in a constructive way."[14]

Enhancements are a normal part of the criminal law process and do not violate equal protection.

The criminal law codes at both the federal and state governments allow for enhancements based on the specific nature of a
crime. "Penalty enhancement statutes are well established in the
law," writes Mark L. Briskman of the Anti-Defamation League.
"In many jurisdictions in America, crimes directed against law-
enforcement officers, public officials, teachers on school grounds
and children carry higher penalties."[15] In 2004, President George
W. Bush signed into law the Identity Theft Penalty Enhancement
Act, which provides for increased penalties for identity theft.[16]

Death-penalty statutes regularly contain aggravating and
mitigating factors that a jury must weigh in order to determine
whether a criminal defendant will receive the death penalty or a
sentence of life in prison. For example, some death-penalty laws
allow as an aggravating factor the fact that a defendant killed a
child or an elderly person. These laws operate differently based
on the particular characteristics of a defendant's crimes. Thus,
penalty-enhancement laws that are triggered when the victim is
selected for particular reasons are not that unusual in American
criminal law.

The California Court of Appeals explained that "the government has a legitimate and even compelling interest in distin-
guishing between acts of violence randomly committed and acts
of violence committed because the victim is a member of a racial,
religious or other protected class."[17] In a later case, the California Court of Appeals reached the same conclusion, saying that
the state had a valid reason to treat the "discriminatory violent
offender" more harshly than the "random violent offender."[18]

Summary

Enhancing penalties for hate crimes is a constitutional, effective, and necessary way to combat the evils of hate crimes. The U.S. Supreme Court has upheld penalty-enhancement laws from a First Amendment challenge by noting that while the First Amendment may protect hateful speech, it does not protect hateful conduct, including violence and true threats. Lower courts have rejected other constitutional challenges to enhanced-penalty hate-crime laws, including challenges based on due process and equal protection. Penalty-enhancement laws are also a common feature of criminal law; stricter penalties are often given to individuals who harm teachers, presidents, police officers, children, and the elderly.

Penalty-Enhancement Laws Violate the Constitution and Further Divide Society

Two individuals commit identical crimes involving assaults against elderly persons. Both individuals select their respective victims because of their advanced age and inflict grievous bodily harm on these victims. One criminal, however, receives a five-year sentence for his crime, while the other receives a much greater penalty because an aggressive prosecutor contends that the assaulter selected his victim not only because of the victim's age but also his religion. In other words, the two criminals receive dramatically different penalties even though they committed the same crime and caused about the same amount of harm. Such a scenario shows not only the unfairness, but the frequently random nature of penalty-enhancement hate-crime laws. A defendant can have a much greater sentence imposed upon him or her because a prosecutor decides that the person harbored discriminatory or hateful thoughts.

Penalty enhancement laws violate the First Amendment by punishing offensive thoughts.

Hate-crimes laws—and particularly those that are called penalty-enhancement laws—violate the First Amendment because they essentially punish a defendant for bigoted thinking. Two people commit the same crime, yet one receives double, triple, or quadruple the amount of punishment because he does not like people of a certain race, religion, or sexual preference. People who commit crimes while uttering racial or religious slurs are therefore punished twice. First, they are punished for the underlying criminal conduct. Then, they are punished for their discriminatory thoughts they verbalize.[1]

Such punishments violate the First Amendment, which protects free speech, no matter how hateful or offensive the expression. Penalty-enhancement laws target the harm caused when a person expresses a hurtful or hateful opinion. As the Wisconsin Supreme Court wrote in Todd Mitchell's case: "Without a doubt the hate crimes statute punishes bigoted thought."[2] In the same ruling, the court went on to note: "The constitution may not embrace or encourage bigoted and hateful thoughts, but it surely protects them."[3] Unfortunately, the U.S. Supreme Court reversed the Wisconsin Supreme Court and failed to appreciate the First Amendment problems with penalty-enhancement provisions.

Some hate-crime laws also may not be drafted narrowly enough to survive First Amendment review. A perfect example was Georgia's law that provided for penalty enhancement if the jury determined beyond a reasonable doubt that a perpetrator intentionally selected his or her victim for the offense "because of bias or prejudice." The Supreme Court of Georgia determined that "because of bias or prejudice" was too broad and vague to withstand constitutional scrutiny. The Georgia court said this law could apply to "a rabid sports fan convicted of uttering terroristic threats to a victim selected for wearing a competing team's baseball cap; a campaign worker convicted of trespassing for defacing a political opponent's yard signs; a performance car fanatic convicted of stealing a Ferrari—any 'bias or prejudice' for or against the selected victim or property, no matter how obscure, whimsical or unrelated to the victim it may be."[4]

Several members of the U.S. House of Representatives objected to the passage of a bill that would have expanded federal law on hate crimes to include perceived sexual orientation, gender identity, gender, or disability. They objected in part because they believed that prosecutors seeking to charge individuals with hate crimes could delve into defendants' associations, reading habits, magazine subscriptions, and other First Amendment-protected activities. Representatives also questioned how far prosecutors

FROM THE BENCH

Wisconsin v. Mitchell, 485 N.W.2d 807, 815–818 (Wis. 1992)

The state admits that this case involves legislation that seeks to address bias related crime. The only definition of "bias" relevant to this case is "prejudice." A statute specifically designed to punish personal prejudice impermissibly infringes upon an individual's First Amendment rights, no matter how carefully or cleverly one words the statute. The hate crime statute enhances the punishment of bigoted criminals because they are bigoted. The statute is directed solely at the subjective motivation of the actor—his or her prejudice. Punishment of one's thought, however repugnant the thought, is unconstitutional....

The hate crimes statute is also unconstitutionally overbroad. A statute is overbroad when it intrudes upon a substantial amount of constitutionally protected activity. Aside from punishing thought, the hate crimes statute also threatens to directly punish an individual's speech and assuredly will have a chilling effect upon free speech....

The use of the defendant's speech, both current and past, as circumstantial evidence to prove the intentional selection, makes it apparent that the statute sweeps protected speech within its ambit and will chill free speech.

The criminal conduct involved in any crime giving rise to the hate crimes penalty enhancer is already punishable. Yet there are numerous instances would go in trying to prove that a defendant acted with sufficient bias. One commentator refers to this as "loose connections between circumstantial evidence . . . and prior associations with bigoted groups."[5]

Penalty-enhancement laws violate other constitutional principles.

Some penalty-enhancement laws may also violate the right, granted by the Sixth Amendment, to a jury trial: "In all criminal prosecutions, the accused shall enjoy the right to a speedy and public trial, by an *impartial jury* of the State and district wherein the crime shall have been committed." (Emphasis added.) This

where this statute can be applied to convert a misdemeanor to a felony merely because of the spoken word. For example, if A strikes B in the face he commits a criminal battery. However, should A add a word such as "nigger," "honky," "Jew," "mick," "kraut," "spic," or "queer," the crime becomes a felony, and A will be punished not for his conduct alone—a misdemeanor—but for using the spoken word. Obviously, the state would respond that the speech is merely an indication that A intentionally selected B because of his particular race or ethnicity, but the fact remains that the necessity to use speech to prove this intentional selection threatens to chill free speech. Opprobrious though the speech may be, an individual must be allowed to utter it without fear of punishment by the state.

And of course the chilling effect goes further than merely deterring an individual from uttering a racial epithet during a battery. Because the circumstantial evidence required to prove the intentional selection is limited only by the relevancy rules of the evidence code, the hate crimes statute will chill every kind of speech.

As disgraceful and deplorable as these and other hate crimes are, the personal prejudices of the attackers are protected by the First Amendment. The constitution may not embrace or encourage bigoted and hateful thoughts, but it surely protects them.

means that a jury, not a judge or any other individual, decides the ultimate fate of a criminal defendant. Hate-crime statutes turn the Sixth Amendment on its head by allowing a judge—instead of a jury—to determine whether a defendant committed a criminal offense. In *Apprendi v. New Jersey* (2000), the U.S. Supreme Court struck down New Jersey's penalty-enhancement provision because it allowed a judge to increase a defendant's sentence after finding that the defendant committed his crime because of racial bias.[6] The Court ruled that the New Jersey penalty scheme violated the Sixth Amendment because a jury was not allowed to determine whether the defendant committed the crime out of racial bias.

The case involved Charles Apprendi Jr., who fired a shot into the home of an African-American family. Apprendi later admitted that he fired the shot because he didn't want black people in the neighborhood. Although he allegedly recanted his statement later, Apprendi faced a much greater sentence because of his bias. While the jury convicted Apprendi of the underlying criminal

QUOTABLE

Scholar Timothy Lynch Testifying Before a U.S. House Subcommittee

Hate crime legislation will take our law too close to the notion of thought crimes. It is true that the hate crime laws that presently exist cover acts, not just thoughts. But once hate crimes laws are on the books, the law enforcement apparatus of the state will be delving into the accused's life and thoughts in order to show that he or she was motivated by bigotry. What kind of books and magazine were found in the home? What internet sites were bookmarked in the computer? Friends and co-workers will be interviewed to discern the accused's politics and worldview. The point here is that such chilling examples of state intrusion are unavoidable because, as noted above, hate crime laws are unnecessary in the first place.

Source: Testimony opposing the *Local Law Enforcement Hate Crimes Protection Act* on April 17, 2007, before a U.S. House subcommittee, p. 36.

conviction, the trial judge determined that the preponderance of evidence showed that Apprendi had acted with a bias motive sufficient to trigger the penalty-enhancement law. The judge then increased Apprendi's sentence from 10 to 20 years because he found that he acted with a discriminatory purpose. The U.S. Supreme Court later rejected the New Jersey law under which the judge sentenced Apprendi because it found that Apprendi's constitutional rights were violated because a jury, not a judge, needed to determine that he had acted with bias and hate and this determination had to be determined as fact beyond a reasonable doubt.

Penalty-enhancement laws also violate the Fifth Amendment guarantee against double jeopardy, which states that no person shall "be subject for the same offense to be twice put in jeopardy of life or limb." This generally means that a person cannot be

FROM THE BENCH

Apprendi v. United States, 530 U.S. 466 (2000)

Other than the fact of a prior conviction, any fact that increases the penalty for a crime beyond the prescribed statutory maximum must be submitted to a jury, and proved beyond a reasonable doubt. With that exception, we endorse the statement of the rule set forth in the concurring opinions in that case: "[I]t is unconstitutional for a legislature to remove from the jury the assessment of facts that increase the prescribed range of penalties to which a criminal defendant is exposed. It is equally clear that such facts must be established by proof beyond a reasonable doubt...."

But it can hardly be said that the potential doubling of one's sentence—from 10 years to 20—has no more than a nominal effect. Both in terms of absolute years behind bars, and because of the more severe stigma attached, the differential here is unquestionably of constitutional significance. When a judge's finding based on a mere preponderance of the evidence authorizes an increase in the maximum punishment, it is appropriately characterized as "a tail which wags the dog of the substantive offense."

tried or punished twice for the same crime. Gregory R. Nearpass noted in the *Albany Law Review* that "the term penalty enhancement is itself only a politically correct way to get around double jeopardy."[7]

The Fifth Amendment's double-jeopardy clause prevents cumulative punishment for the same offense. Despite this, penalty-enhancement provisions allow a defendant to be punished more than once for the same offense. "It is no wonder why legislators, when drafting their respective hate crime legislation, have used the word 'penalty-enhancement' instead of 'cumulative punishment.' "[8]

Penalty-enhancement hate crime laws balkanize individuals.

Hate-crime legislation comes from good intentions. Such laws, however, cause more harm than good. They actually emphasize differences between people rather than allow victims and defendants to be treated equally under the law. Douglas Lee explains: "By their nature, hate-crime laws single out minorities and require prosecutors to treat crimes against minorities differently than crimes against others. At the same time that women, blacks and gays seek equal treatment under the law and in society, hate-crime laws perpetuate and encourage isolating categorizations. At the same time that minorities seek to eradicate distinctions based on bias and prejudice, hate-crime laws hold minorities before juries as victims who are defined predominantly by their race, religion and sexual orientation."[9]

A related problem with hate-crime laws that enhance penalties for certain crimes is that other "minority" groups are left out and will feel marginalized. What if, for example, a person is targeted for crime because of their weight, medical condition, height, political affiliations, union membership, skin condition, or profession? A person is not less deserving of protection simply because they were targeted for one of these reasons than because of their race, religion, or sexual orientation. A well-meaning

response to this undeniable problem is that government officials can expand a hate-crime law to provide a penalty enhancer
for other types of people. As Timothy Lynch noted in testimony
before a House subcommittee in 2007, however, "if all victim
groups are included, the hate crime category will be no different
than 'ordinary' criminal law."[10] A related problem is that hate-
crime penalty enhancers may actually harm the victims. Susan
Gellman writes: "Society wishes to protect them [hate-crime vic-
tims] because they are more helpless than others; the protection
is beneficial, but it reinforces the belief of weakness."[11]

The better solution is to have effective enforcement of *existing* laws. For example, if a person assaults someone, then the
person should be charged and, hopefully, convicted of the crime
of assault. If a person vandalizes a neighbor's property, he or
she should be prosecuted and convicted of that crime. There is
no need to tack on additional charges that are constitutionally
problematic.

Penalty-enhancement laws are difficult to enforce and do not deter future crime.

Penalty-enhancement laws present special problems in the law
enforcement and prosecution context. It is often very difficult
to determine beyond a reasonable doubt whether an offender
was motivated by hate or some other reason. Karen Franklin
notes that "people may hurl racist, sexist, or antigay epithets
in the heat of a confrontation that is rooted more in tangible
concerns."[12] For example, imagine that motorist A is cut off by
motorist B, which leads to a physical confrontation. A and B are
of different races. A slugs B, and, in the midst of the struggle,
racial slurs are uttered. If A is prosecuted for assault, will the
prosecutor seek an enhanced charge because of alleged racial
bias? What if it turns out A and B had dated the same woman
and that turned out to be the primary motivation for the dislike
between the two? A may have simply been very angry at B for the
car incident or primarily been mad because he had a bad day at

work. "The inherent subjectivity of this process invites arbitrary and uneven application of the penalty enhancement," Franklin writes.[13] Prosecutors and defense attorneys have admitted that such laws are very difficult to enforce and may cause more problems than they are worth. Ed Shettle, an assistant criminal district attorney in Jefferson County, Texas, told the *Beaumont Enterprise*: "It's not a practical tool. It's a feel-good deal. Anytime you charge that offense, it has political connotations. And it would be extremely easy to get a hung jury."[14] A defense attorney told the paper that these laws require prosecutors to meet an even more difficult burden of showing why a defendant selected his or her victim: "It is hard enough to prove the intent of why somebody selected a particular victim. But then to prove the intent of why somebody selected a particular victim would really involve delving into the mind of an individual. And that's a hard thing to do."[15]

Another problem with penalty-enhancement laws is that there is virtually no evidence to suggest that such laws actually deter future crimes. Franklin explains, "There is currently little evidence that, in and of themselves, they will lead to a reduction in intergroup conflict." She goes on to say, "publicity surrounding their enforcement may frequently lead to increases in both true and false reporting of hate crimes."[16]

Summary

Criminal law should punish offenders for their criminal conduct—not for their thoughts. A person who commits murder, assault, or any other crime should be prosecuted for that crime. Prosecutors and courts should not increase sentences simply because a defendant harbors discriminatory thoughts. Punishing prejudicial thinking is a fundamental violation of the First Amendment, which protects free speech, no matter how repugnant.

Hate-crime laws potentially violate other constitutional rights. Hate-crime laws may violate the Sixth and Fourteenth

Amendment rights of a criminal defendant if a judge, rather than a jury, imposes a penalty enhancer without a finding of beyond a reasonable doubt—the traditional criminal law standard. These laws also raise troubling double-jeopardy concerns because the defendant is, in effect, being punished twice for the same crime.

More practically, hate-crime penalty-enhancement laws present very difficult enforcement concerns. It is very hard to show that a crime was inspired principally or substantively by racial, religious, or anti-gay bias. Oftentimes, the motivation for the crime will be something not relating to the identifiable characteristics of the defendant. Finally, penalty-enhancement laws have not been proven to be an actual deterrent to future hate crimes, leading commentator Edward Rothstein to ask: "Is it possible that one of the best ways to eliminate hate crimes is to jettison the concept itself?"[17]

The Display of a Noose is a Hate Crime and Noose-Display Laws are Constitutional

On December 4, 2006, a white student at Jena High School in Louisiana named Justin Barker was beaten by a group of six black teenagers. He was taken to the emergency room and released the same day, but later sued the six students, the school, and others involved in the incident. Criminal charges were brought against the six African-American students. The attack on Barker, however, was not an isolated incident; several events preceding the assault have since been linked to an escalation of racial tensions between black and white students at the school. In addition to two physical confrontations between black and white students and the destruction by fire of the main high school building, hangman's nooses were hung from a tree in the high school courtyard after black students sat under it—a place where only white students typically hung out. According to some

Above, demonstrators march through the streets of the Louisiana town of Jena to protest the prosecution of six black high school students for beating a white classmate.

accounts, the so-called "Jena Six" reacted *after* the nooses were hung. The Jena Six incident later led to a series of other disturbing noose incidents around the country.[1]

The hangman's noose—perhaps the most virulent symbol in history of racial violence—resurfaced later in the Jena case, after activists and civil-rights advocates marched in Jena to protest the perceived injustice to the six students. One young man displayed two nooses from his pickup truck as he drove past civil-rights marches in Alexandria, Louisiana—a city about 30 miles away. He allegedly displayed the nooses as a tool of intimidation. He later faced federal charges for this, as he was charged with a hate crime.[2]

Sadly, the Jena case is not the only one of its kind. Since then, there has been a rash of noose-display cases across the country, not only in public schools but also in places of business. In High Point, North Carolina, African-American workers at Henredon Furniture Industries were subjected to a barrage of racial harassment, including the display of hangmen's nooses. The Equal Employment Opportunity Commission (EEOC) filed a class-action lawsuit on behalf of many workers at the plant. The EEOC

(continues on page 45)

QUOTABLE

President George W. Bush

Our nation has come a long way toward building a more perfect union. Yet as past injustices have become distant memories, there's a risk that our society may lose sight of the real suffering that took place. One symbol of that suffering is the noose. Recently, there have been a number of media reports about nooses being displayed. These disturbing reports have resulted in heightened racial tensions in many communities. They have revealed that some Americans do not understand why the sight of a noose causes such a visceral reaction among so many people.

For decades, the noose played a central part in a campaign of violence and fear against African Americans. Fathers were dragged from their homes in the dark of the night before the eyes of their terrified children. Summary executions were held by torchlight in front of hateful crowds. In many cases, law enforcement officers responsible for protecting the victims were complicit in . . . their deaths. For generations of African Americans, the noose was more than a tool of murder; it was a tool of intimidation that conveyed a sense of powerlessness to millions.

The era of rampant lynching is a shameful chapter in American history. The noose is not a symbol of prairie justice, but of gross injustice. Displaying one is not a harmless prank. And lynching is not a word to be mentioned in jest. As a civil society, we must understand that noose displays and lynching jokes are deeply offensive. They are wrong. And they have no place in America today.

Source: White House news release, "President Bush Celebrates African American History Month," February 12, 2008. http://www.whitehouse.gov/news/releases/2008/02/20080 212–3.html.

Hangman's nooses, as pictured above, are often seen as symbols of racial oppression in the United States. The display of such nooses was condemned by President George W. Bush and the U.S. Congress and has been outlawed in many states. In a 2007 report, the NAACP wrote that "the hangman's noose is a symbol of the racist, segregation-era violence enacted on blacks."

From the Legislature: U.S. Senate Resolution on Noose Displays

Expressing the sense of the Senate that the hanging of nooses should be thoroughly investigated by Federal, State, and local law enforcement authorities and that any criminal violations should be vigorously prosecuted.

Whereas, in the fall of 2007, nooses have been found hanging in or near a high school in North Carolina, a Home Depot store in New Jersey, a school playground in Louisiana, the campus of the University of Maryland, a factory in Houston, Texas, and on the door of a professor's office at Columbia University;

Whereas the Southern Poverty Law Center has recorded between 40 and 50 suspected hate crimes involving nooses since September 2007;

Whereas, since 2001, the Equal Employment Opportunity Commission has filed more than 30 lawsuits that involve the displaying of nooses in places of employment;

Whereas nooses are reviled by many Americans as symbols of racism and of lynchings that were once all too common;

Whereas, according to Tuskegee Institute, more than 4,700 people were lynched between 1882 and 1959 in a campaign of terror led by the Ku Klux Klan;

Whereas the number of victims killed by lynching in the history of the United States exceeds the number of people killed in the horrible attack on Pearl Harbor (2,333 dead) and Hurricane Katrina (1,836 dead) combined; and

Whereas African-Americans, as well as Italian, Jewish, and Mexican-Americans, have comprised the vast majority of lynching victims, and, by erasing the terrible symbols of the past, we can continue to move forward on issues of race in the United States: Now, therefore, be it

Resolved, That it is the sense of the Senate that—

(1) the hanging of nooses is a reprehensible act when used for the purpose of intimidation and, under certain circumstances, can be criminal;

(2) incidents involving the hanging of a noose should be investigated thoroughly by Federal, State, and local law enforcement, and all private entities and individuals should be encouraged to cooperate with any such investigation; and

(3) any criminal violations involving the hanging of nooses should be vigorously prosecuted.

Source: SR 396, 110th Congress, December 14, 2007. http://www.govtrack.us/congress/record.xpd?id=110-s20071214–50.

(continued from page 42)
secured a nearly half-million dollar settlement on behalf of the aggrieved workers.[3] "Racial harassment continues to be a problem," said EEOC Regional Attorney John Hendrickson from the Chicago district office at a February 2007 meeting. "Nooses are still hung from factory piping, placed in lunch boxes and drawn around the necks of photographs of black children."[4]

Certain types of symbolic speech can enrage, inflame, and outrage observers. The burning of an American flag roils many people in this country. Another particularly noxious form of symbolic speech involves the display of a noose—a tool or symbol of racial oppression in this country. The NAACP wrote in its 2007 report "State of Emergency" that the noose "is an unmistakable symbol of violence and terror that whites used to demonstrate their hatred for blacks."[5]

The problem is so well known that President George W. Bush addressed it during a February 2008 White House conference.

In response to these noose displays, both houses of Congress acted to pass resolutions urging law enforcement personnel at the federal, state, and local level to examine noose displays "more thoroughly." A Senate resolution urged that "incidents involving the hanging of a noose should be investigated thoroughly by Federal, State, and local law enforcement, and all private entities and individuals should be encouraged to cooperate with any such investigation."[6]

More and more states have responded to noose displays with legislation.

In response to these recent noxious incidents, several state legislatures have introduced bills criminalizing the display of nooses. Several states, including Connecticut, Louisiana, and New York, have adopted such legislation. In May 2008, Connecticut amended a hate-crime law by adding a noose-display section that provided: "Any person who places a noose or a simulation thereof on any public property, or on any private property without the written consent of the owner, and with intent to intimidate or harass any other person on account of religion, national origin, alienage, color, race, sex, sexual orientation, blindness or physical disability, shall be in violation" of the law.[7]

Connecticut Governor M. Jodi Rell signed the measure into law on May 7, 2008. "Connecticut simply will not tolerate bigotry or racism," Rell said in a statement. "Let this bill send that message loud and clear. Using a noose—a symbol of the racially motivated lynchings during the late 19th and first half of the 20th century—to intimidate anyone because of their race or any other characteristic is a repugnant and cowardly act. No one should be subject to that kind of treatment."[8]

New York passed a similar bill, also in May 2008. The New York measure amends an existing aggravated-harassment law to bar the etching, painting, drawing, or display of a noose. It provides that such action is a crime unless the person has the permission of the private or public property owner.

New York Governor David A. Paterson signed his state's measure into law on the same day that Governor Rell signed Connecticut's. "It is sad that in these modern times there remains

THE LETTER OF THE LAW

From the State Legislature of New York

§ 240.31. Aggravated harassment in the first degree

A person is guilty of aggravated harassment in the first degree when with intent to harass, annoy, threaten or alarm another person, because of a belief or perception regarding such person's race, color, national origin, ancestry, gender, religion, religious practice, age, disability or sexual orientation, regardless of whether the belief or perception is correct, he or she:...

Etches, paints, draws upon or otherwise places or displays a noose, commonly exhibited as a symbol of racism and intimidation, on any building or other real property, public or private, owned by any person, firm or corporation or any public agency or instrumentality, without express permission of the owner or operator of such building or real property.

Source: NY CLS Penal § 240.31 (2008)

a need to address the problem of individuals who use nooses as a means of threat and intimidation," Paterson, the state's first African-American governor, said in a statement. "But it is a reality and if we ignore it we would be derelict in our duty. The Legislature has given voice to the revulsion that such incidents inspire in all of us."[9]

In July 2008, Louisiana Governor Bobby Jindal signed into law a measure to outlaw the display of a noose with the intent to intimidate. The law provides for a criminal penalty of up to one year in jail and/or a $5,000 fine. The Louisiana law provides: "It shall be unlawful for any person, with the intent to intimidate any person or group of persons, to etch, paint or draw or otherwise place or display a hangman's noose on the property of another, a highway, or other public place."[10]

Noose display laws are supported by U.S. Supreme Court precedent.

U.S. Supreme Court case law supports legislation that bans the display of a noose with the intent to intimidate. The laws do not ban nooses in and of themselves; rather they ban the use or display of a noose with the intent to intimidate or threaten others. In *Virginia v. Black*, the U.S. Supreme Court upheld a similar law that banned cross-burnings done with the intent to intimidate.[11] The Virginia law provided: "It shall be unlawful for any person or persons, with the intent of intimidating any person or group of persons, to burn, or cause to be burned, a cross on the property of another, a highway or other public place."

The high court reasoned that cross-burnings done with the intent to intimidate others constitute true threats unprotected by the First Amendment.

The *Virginia v. Black* opinion explains why many of the noose-display laws, rather than imposing a flat ban, contain language requiring that the display or drawing involve the "intent to intimidate." The Supreme Court reasoned that not all cross burnings were necessarily done with such intent and, thus, may not qualify as true threats. Justice Sandra Day O'Connor explained:

The First Amendment permits Virginia to outlaw cross burn-ings done with the intent to intimidate because burning a cross is a particularly virulent form of intimidation. Instead of prohibiting all intimidating messages, Virginia may choose to regulate this subset of intimidating messages in light of cross burning's long and pernicious history as a signal of impending violence. Thus, just as a State may regulate only that obscenity which is the most obscene due to its prurient content, so too may a State choose to prohibit only those forms of intimida-tion that are most likely to inspire fear of bodily harm.[12]

The same logic applies to noose displays. States may pass laws regulating such displays because they are forms of intimidation directly linked to the most pernicious types of racial violence.

Robert M. O'Neil, founding director of the Thomas Jef-ferson Center for the Protection of Free Expression, has said he believes that the Court's decision in *Virginia v. Black* provides

FROM THE BENCH

Virginia v. Black, 538 U.S. 343, 359–360 (2003)

"True threats" encompass those statements where the speaker means to commu-nicate a serious expression of an intent to commit an act of unlawful violence to a particular individual or group of individuals. The speaker need not actually intend to carry out the threat. Rather, a prohibition on true threats "protect[s] individuals from the fear of violence" and "from the disruption that fear engenders," in addi-tion to protecting people "from the possibility that the threatened violence will occur." Intimidation in the constitutionally proscribable sense of the word is a type of true threat, where a speaker directs a threat to a person or group of persons with the intent of placing the victim in fear of bodily harm or death. Respondents do not contest that some cross burnings fit within this meaning of intimidating speech, and rightly so. As noted in Part II, supra, the history of cross burning in this country shows that cross burning is often intimidating, intended to create a pervasive fear in victims that they are a target of violence.

support for a noose-display law that singles out displays made with intent to intimidate. "I am unable to offer a principled distinction between the burning cross and the noose display," he said. "There is obviously no major distinction between the noose and the burning cross in *Black*. Once the Court started down that path in *Black,* the drawing of a sharp, clear distinction has to be based on something exclusive or unique."[13]

Supporters of noose-display laws point out that nooses and cross burnings share a similar shameful history. In fact, nooses may be seen as worse because they were the actual tool used to lynch so many African Americans and other minorities.

Summary

The hangman's noose was used to lynch and kill people, usually members of racial minorities. It epitomizes an ugly era of rampant segregation, racial violence, and discrimination. Noose displays often convey messages of threats, intimidation, and racism. When a person displays a noose, he or she often does so to threaten another person. The First Amendment does not protect true threats. The display of a noose with an intent to intimidate is not protected speech; rather it is unprotected conduct. More and more legislatures are responding to this real problem of harassing noose displays. Nothing in the Constitution or Bill of Rights prevents states from attempting to protect people from these acts of intimidation.

Banning the Display of Nooses Is Unnecessary and Unconstitutional

The presidential election of 2008 elicited an enormous, and impassioned, voter turnout. During the campaign, more people were energized to express their support or criticism for Democratic Senator Barack Obama or Republican Senator John McCain than had been seen in recent presidential elections. In their fervor to express their political opinions, numerous individuals hung effigies of the various candidates. For example, individuals hung effigies of Obama, McCain, and Alaskan Governor Sarah Palin, the Republican vice-presidential candidate. Many of the individuals did not intend the use of nooses to convey direct threats or to intimidate other would-be voters. They simply used the noose to convey their strong political opposition to a particular political figure. While we may disagree or disapprove of this type of obnoxious, in-your-face expression, the fact remains this is an example of political speech—the core type of speech the First Amendment was designed to protect.

The First Amendment protects offensive speech.

"If there is a bedrock principle underlying the First Amendment, it is that the government may not prohibit the expression of an idea simply because it finds it offensive or disagreeable."[1] Justice William Brennan wrote these words in a controversial 1989 U.S. Supreme Court decision that upheld the right of a person to burn the American flag as a form of political protest.

The Supreme Court's decision in that case, while infuriating to those who would never want to see the American flag desecrated, was not an unusual decision in light of the fact that American law protects even the most offensive displays of free speech. A federal court has protected the right of the Ku Klux Klan to march in a predominately Jewish town to express its disfavored political viewpoints. The federal appeals court ruled

FROM THE BENCH

Skokie v. Nationalist Socialist Party, 373 N.E.2d 21 (Ill. 1978)

The display of the swastika, as offensive to the principles of a free nation as the memories it recalls may be, is symbolic political speech intended to convey to the public the beliefs of those who display it. It does not, in our opinion, fall within the definition of "fighting words," and that doctrine cannot be used here to overcome the heavy presumption against the constitutional validity of a prior restraint.

Nor can we find that the swastika, while not representing fighting words, is nevertheless so offensive and peace threatening to the public that its display can be enjoined. We do not doubt that the sight of this symbol is abhorrent to the Jewish citizens of Skokie, and that the survivors of the Nazi persecutions, tormented by their recollections, may have strong feelings regarding its display. Yet it is entirely clear that this factor does not justify enjoining defendants' speech.

that the marchers could even display the swastika—the symbol of Nazism and a reminder of the Jewish Holocaust that occurred under the Nazis—in the predominately Jewish village.[2] The U.S. Supreme Court ruled in *Hustler v. Falwell* that pornographer Larry Flynt could make outlandish statements about religious figure Jerry Falwell.[3] The Supreme Court ruled in *Brandenburg v. Ohio* that Ku Klux Klan leader Clarence Brandenburg could utter vile racial and anti-Semitic remarks to a group of klansmen.[4]

Displaying a hangman's noose, while offensive to many, is also protected as free speech. Mike Riggs writes that the noose's "negative cultural significance is not sufficient justification to ban it on public property."[5] Political scientist and law professor Carol Swain explains: "A hanging noose is a chilling symbol, but it only becomes a hate crime when it is being used to lynch a human being. Most likely, the U.S. Supreme Court would consider a noose as protected speech under the First Amendment."[6]

Singling out a symbol can constitute viewpoint discrimination.

The most fundamental of all First Amendment principles provides that the government may not ban a certain type of free speech simply because of its viewpoint. Justice Thurgood Marshall once wrote that if "the First Amendment means anything, above all else, it means that the government may not discriminate against speech because of its message, ideas, subject matter or content."[7] In *Tinker v. Des Moines Independent Community School District*, the U.S. Supreme Court ruled that public school officials in Iowa could not prohibit students from wearing black armbands because that symbol was associated with a particular viewpoint.[8] The school officials selectively targeted black armbands but allowed students to wear Iron Crosses and political campaign buttons. Similarly, an anti-noose-display law selectively singles out a particular symbol (a hangman's noose) and runs the danger of targeting certain forms of political viewpoints or speech.

In *R.A.V. v. City of St. Paul*, the U.S. Supreme Court invalidated a St. Paul, Minnesota, ordinance that prohibited certain forms of hate crimes based on certain criteria. The ordinance provided: "Whoever places on public or private property a symbol, object, appellation, characterization or graffiti, including, but not limited to, a burning cross or Nazi swastika, which one knows or has reasonable grounds to know arouses anger, alarm or resentment in others on the basis of race, color, creed, religion or gender, commits disorderly conduct and shall be guilty of a misdemeanor."[9]

Justice Antonin Scalia pointed out that the St. Paul ordinance prohibited only certain displays—those done to anger or alarm others on the basis of "race, color, creed, religion or gender." It did not cover displays targeting people because of their "political affiliation, union membership, or homosexuality." The problem

FROM THE BENCH

R.A.V. v. City of St. Paul, 505 U.S. 377 (1992)

St. Paul has not singled out an especially offensive mode of expression—it has not, for example, selected for prohibition only those fighting words that communicate ideas in a threatening (as opposed to a merely obnoxious) manner. Rather, it has proscribed fighting words of whatever manner that communicate messages of racial, gender, or religious intolerance. Selectivity of this sort creates the possibility that the city is seeking to handicap the expression of particular ideas. . . .

The dispositive question in this case, therefore, is whether content discrimination is reasonably necessary to achieve St. Paul's compelling interests; it plainly is not. An ordinance not limited to the favored topics, for example, would have precisely the same beneficial effect. In fact the only interest distinctively served by the content limitation is that of displaying the city council's special hostility towards the particular biases thus singled out. That is precisely what the First Amendment forbids. The politicians of St. Paul are entitled to express that hostility—but not through the means of imposing unique limitations upon speakers who (however benightedly) disagree.

with this selective banning of burning crosses or swastikas was that it raised the problem of viewpoint discrimination. "The First Amendment does not permit St. Paul to impose special prohibitions on those speakers who express views on disfavored subjects," he wrote.[10] The decision means that a noose-display measure must not selectively prohibit displays because of a victim's race, gender, or national origin. It must prohibit any noose display that truly constitutes a true threat to another individual.[11]

It is difficult to determine intent in displaying a noose.

Noose-display laws raise not only troubling constitutional concerns but also a host of practical problems as well. A noose-display law that prohibits those displays that are done with the required intent to intimidate presents the problem of determining the intent of someone who posted a noose. Imagine a person hangs a noose around an effigy of a political figure; some people may believe that the noose display was intended as a sign of racism or racial threat. The person displaying a noose, however, merely holds strong opinions against the political figure. What if a person displays a noose during the Halloween season that some interpret as a threat, but the real purpose behind the noose was simply someone acting (even if wrongly) in the Halloween spirit? Such noose displays may not even qualify as offensive, and hardly as a tool of intimidation. Marjorie Esman, executive director of the Louisiana American Civil Liberties Union, questioned whether Louisiana's noose-display law is constitutional. She said the law was "overbroad since no one can know what the intent (of the person who places the noose) is; it does not meet constitutional standards."[12] As the Baton Rouge, Louisiana, newspaper the *Advocate* editorialized: "Some displays of nooses, such as those used in museum exhibits, Halloween haunted houses and in pep rallies where effigies of opposing mascots are strung up, are not offensive. . . . But just who decides when intimidation was intended?"[13]

What symbols would be next?

If nooses become outlawed symbols, one has to wonder what other symbols would be removed from the marketplace of ideas. What if a person wishes to express their Southern pride and heritage by displaying a Confederate flag? What if another person wishes to express his support for the cause of racial advancement and civil rights by wearing a Malcolm X T-shirt? To some, a Confederate flag or a Malcolm X T-shirt are racially divisive and offensive. What if the banning of symbols extended to people wishing to express their support for a certain immigration policy by waving a Mexican flag or by wearing an English-only button? Once society starts removing symbols from the public discourse, there is no logical ending point.

The U.S. Supreme Court recognized this slippery slope in the aforementioned flag-burning decision, *Texas v. Johnson*. Justice Brennan, writing for the majority, wondered what other symbols would receive special protection under the law:

> To conclude that the government may permit designated symbols to be used to communicate only a limited set of messages would be to enter territory having no discernible or defensible boundaries. Could the government, on this theory, prohibit the burning of state flags? Of copies of the Presidential seal? Of the Constitution? In evaluating these choices under the First Amendment, how would we decide which symbols were sufficiently special to warrant this unique status? To do so, we would be forced to consult our own political preferences, and impose them on the citizenry, in the very way that the First Amendment forbids us to do.[14]

Summary

Laws banning noose displays may be well intentioned, but the logic behind such laws is fatally flawed. A law singling out a specific symbol—often associated with particular viewpoints— contradicts fundamental First Amendment principles. Above all else, the First Amendment forbids viewpoint discrimination. Laws that specifically prohibit a specific symbol often discriminate against particular viewpoints. Even if many of us disagree with those viewpoints, or find them repugnant, such expression *must* be tolerated in a free society.

Furthermore, not all noose displays are threatening enough to remove constitutional protection. Many noose displays may be displayed on public property or on private property with the permission of the property owner. Many noose displays are not targeting a specific individual or even a specific group of individuals. They are simply a form of unpopular political speech that deserves the protection of the First Amendment. As the *New York Post* editorialized: "The noose is a hateful symbol of a shameful chapter in American history. But responding to it by doing violence to the First Amendment gives the bigots a dangerous victory."[15]

The Federal Government Must Do More to Protect Victims of Hate Crimes Based on Sexual Orientation

Available data indicates that violence based on sexual orientation and gender identity bias is a significant portion of violent hate crimes overall and are characterized by levels of physical violence that in some cases exceed those present in other cases.

Human Rights First (2008) [1]

By all accounts, Matthew Shepard was a happy student at the University of Wyoming in Laramie. An openly gay young man, the diminutive Shepard had just attended a meeting of a lesbian, gay, bisexual, and transgendered association. After the meeting, he went to a bar to have a beer, and he met two men who claimed to be gay. They lured Shepard to their truck, where they abducted him and took him to a more rural area. They beat him with a pistol, burned him with cigarettes, and then tied him

Pictured, Matthew Shepard, the young man who was murdered because of his sexual orientation, during his days at Casper College. He later attended the University of Wyoming.

to a split-rail fence to die. A bicyclist who later saw Shepard on the fence told police he thought he saw a scarecrow. Emergency personnel rushed the comatose Shepard to a hospital; he never regained consciousness and died a few days later.[2]

The attack inspired an award-winning play and film, *The Laramie Project*. It also inspired a call to toughen hate-crime laws to protect the gay and lesbian community, a group that often faces not only rampant discrimination but, occasionally, outright physical violence and murder. In October 2008, 10 years after Shepard's murder, groups around the country held events seeking to raise public awareness about the problems of intolerance that gays and lesbians face in society.

Perhaps more tragically, Matthew Shepard is far from being the only openly gay person to be killed because of his sexual orientation. In February 2008, a 15-year-old student in Oxnard, California, was shot by a classmate. Many believe the shooting was related to the victim's sexual orientation, as the victim had endured much harassment from other students at school.[3] These vicious assaults, and many others like them, show the need for legislation that deals with hate crimes committed against gays and lesbians. Congress needs to pass the Matthew Shepard Act.

Hate-crime laws including sexual orientation protects a historically excluded group.

Hate-crime legislation protects an insular minority that has faced discrimination and danger for centuries. In the American colonial era, people could be executed for sodomy. For much of the twentieth century, homosexuality was considered a mental illness.[4] The term "gay-bashing" did not appear out of thin air. Rather, it was coined to address a dangerous phenomenon. In the 1940s and 1950s, the federal government through the House Un-American Activities Committee and the Senate's McCarthy Hearings (named after Senator Joseph McCarthy, an ardent anti-Communist), considered homosexuals to be potential national security threats. In the 1950s, President Dwight D. Eisenhower issued an executive order listing "sexual perversion" as a reason to deny a person federal employment.[5]

Despite gains made in recent decades, many gays and lesbians still face discrimination in the private workplace. Every state has an anti-discrimination law that prevents employers from firing or demoting individuals based on their race, religion, or gender. Most states, as of this writing, do not have laws that protect people from being fired for their sexual orientation. For more than a decade, some members of Congress have attempted to pass legislation that would protect this often-overlooked minority. Representative John Conyers explained that in drafting the

Proposed Legislation: *Local Law Enforcement Hate Crimes Prevention Act*—Congressional Findings

Congress makes the following findings:

(1) The incidence of violence motivated by the actual or perceived race, religion, national origin, gender, sexual orientation, gender identity, or disability of the victim poses a serious national problem.

(2) Such violence disrupts the tranquility and safety of communities and is deeply divisive.

(3) State and local authorities are now and will continue to be responsible for prosecuting the overwhelming majority of violent crimes in the United States, including violent crimes motivated by bias. These authorities can carry out their responsibilities more effectively with greater Federal assistance.

(4) Existing Federal law is inadequate to address this problem.

(5) A prominent characteristic of a violent crime motivated by bias is that it devastates not just the actual victim and the family and friends of the victim, but frequently savages the community sharing the traits that caused the victim to be selected.

(6) Such violence substantially affects interstate commerce in many ways, including the following:

Matthew Shepard Act, "we are not giving anybody superior protection; we are bringing in a group that has been excluded for a long time."[6]

Hate crimes against gays and lesbians are increasing and underreported.

An alarmingly high percentage of reported hate crimes under the Hate Crime Statistics Act of 1990 are committed because of a victim's sexual orientation. For several years, more than 16% of reported hate crimes involved sexual orientation. In 1999, Eric Holder, then a federal prosecutor and now the U.S. attorney

(A) The movement of members of targeted groups is impeded, and members of such groups are forced to move across State lines to escape the incidence or risk of such violence.

(B) Members of targeted groups are prevented from purchasing goods and services, obtaining or sustaining employment, or participating in other commercial activity.

(C) Perpetrators cross State lines to commit such violence.

(D) Channels, facilities, and instrumentalities of interstate commerce are used to facilitate the commission of such violence.

(E) Such violence is committed using articles that have traveled in interstate commerce....

(9) Federal jurisdiction over certain violent crimes motivated by bias enables Federal, State, and local authorities to work together as partners in the investigation and prosecution of such crimes.

(10) The problem of crimes motivated by bias is sufficiently serious, widespread, and interstate in nature as to warrant Federal assistance to States, local jurisdictions, and Indian tribes.

Source: S. 1105—*Local Law Enforcement Hate Crimes Prevention Act of 2007.* http://thomas. loc.gov/cgi-bin/query/z?c110:S.1105.

general, testified before Congress: "Violent hate crimes committed because of the victim's sexual orientation . . . pose a serious problem for our nation. From the statistics gathered by the federal government and by private organizations as well, we know that a significant number of hate crimes based on the sexual orientation of a victim occur every year in this country."[7] Senator Arlen Specter of Pennsylvania agreed with the assessment, stating in the Senate Judiciary Committee hearing: "There has been a special upsurge in violence against individuals because of sexual orientation—really sort of shocking as to what has occurred."[8] Statistics compiled by the Federal Bureau of Investigation pursuant to the Hate Crime Statistics Act of 1990 show there were more than 1,260 incidents involving crimes because of sexual orientation in 2007.[9] The FBI explained that of the reported 7,621 single-bias incidents, "16.6 percent were motivated by sexual-orientation bias."[10]

Legal commentator Kathleen Bantley explains: "By not including sexual orientation as a protected category, it perpetuates the idea that gays and lesbians can be treated harshly just because they are gay."[11]

Judy Shepard, the mother of Matthew Shepard, has testified before Congress and various state legislatures on the need for hate-crime legislation and the need for it to cover crimes because of a person's sexual orientation.

The statistics of hate crimes against people based on sexual orientation do not begin to adequately describe the rampant discrimination that such individuals face in an often-intolerant society. The statistics also do not convey the scope of the problem because many gay and lesbian people fail to report the hate crimes that have been committed against them. As professor Jack McDevitt testified before Congress in 2007: "Lastly, the reluctance to report hate-crime victimization is an essential factor to understand in working with victims of anti-homosexual hate crime."[12] A U.S. House of Representatives report on the need for further federal legislation to combat hate crimes noted that

QUOTABLE

Judy Shepard's Testimony Before the Senate Judiciary Committee

On October 12th, Matt was pronounced dead. And I can assure opponents of this legislation firsthand, it was not words or thoughts but violent actions that killed my son. Matt is no longer with us today because the men who killed him learned to hate.

Somehow and somewhere they received the message that the lives of gay people are not as worthy of respect, dignity, and honor as the lives of other people. They were given the impression that society condoned or at least was indifferent to violence against gay and lesbian Americans.

Today we have it within our power to send a very different message than the one received by the people who killed my son. It is time to stop living in denial and to address a real problem that is destroying families like mine and James Byrd Jr.'s, and Billie Jack Gaither's and many others across America.

It is time to pass the Hate Crimes Prevention Act. Opponents of this bill will say that the men and women who killed Matt will be punished with life in prison or even the death penalty. What more can a new law do, they ask? Maybe nothing in this case, but we will never know, will we? Perhaps these murderers would have gotten a message that this country does not tolerate hate-motivating violence. Maybe I would not have to be here today talking about how my son was savagely beaten, tied to a fence, and left to die in freezing temperatures....

Today, I not only speak for myself, but for all the victims of hate crimes we will never hear about. Since 1991, hate crimes have nearly doubled. In 1997, the FBI's most recent reporting period [showed] race-related hate crimes were by far the most common, representing nearly 60 percent of all cases. Hate crimes based on religion represented 17 percent more cases. And hate crimes against gay, lesbian and bisexual Americans increased by 8 percent or 14 percent of all hate crimes recorded.

We need to decide what kind of nation we want to be, one that treats all people with dignity and respect, or one that allows some people and their family members to be marginalized. I know personally that there is a hole in my existence. I will never again experience Matt's laugh, his wonderful hugs, his stories.

I know Matt would be very disappointed if I gave up. He would be disappointed in all of us if we give up.

Source: Judy Shepard, speaking before the Senate Judiciary Committee, "Hearing on Hate Crimes," May 11, 1999.

"many victims of anti-lesbian, anti-gay and anti-transgender incidents do not report the crimes to local law enforcement officials."[13] The majority view in the House Judiciary Committee quoted a law enforcement official from Texas that "despite under-reporting, the trend in State statistics shows that gays and lesbians are increasingly the targets of crime."[14]

Hate-crime laws that cover victims based on sexual orientation do not threaten religious freedom.

Opponents of hate-crime legislation that includes sexual orientation as a protected category sound the alarm that somehow such laws will threaten religious freedom. They claim that a pastor quoting biblical passages condemning homosexuality could be subject to official investigation for allegedly intimidating others and perhaps causing hate crimes to occur. Such claims are farfetched. The House Judiciary Committee explained that proposed federal hate-crimes legislation, the Matthew Shepard Act, would not infringe on religious freedom rights. It informs that an amendment was adopted to add "a rule of construction that further clarifies that freedom of religious and other expression protected under the First Amendment is in no way impaired."[15]

Religious liberty scholar Charles C. Haynes explains that such claims are not well founded. He explains that the broad protections of the First Amendment free-speech clause—"Congress shall make no law . . . abridging the freedom of speech"—would provide protection to those who express their religious-based opposition to gays and lesbians. "Moreover, the danger to hate-crime laws to free expression isn't supported by our experience of living under such laws," he writes. "Under the present hate-crime laws (32 of which include sexual orientation), nobody has been convicted of a hate crime solely on the basis of thought, belief or speech."[16]

As Haynes aptly observes, "More than threats to free speech, it is the mainstream acceptance of gay, lesbian, bisexual and transgender people that many Christian conservative groups most fear. That's why victory bells on one side are answered by alarm bells on the other."[17]

The federal government must ensure the protection of gays and lesbians.

It is an undeniable historical fact that gays and lesbians have been a disadvantaged group for centuries, if not thousands of years. The U.S. government was actively hostile to gays and lesbians for much of the twentieth century. It is imperative for the federal government to ensure that gays and lesbians are given the full protection of the federal law. Just as the federal government was needed to enforce the civil rights of African Americans during the 1960s, federal enforcement is necessary in states hostile to gays and lesbians. As Senator Arlen Specter said during a federal hate-crimes congressional hearing in 1999: "And make no mistake about it, when the federal government is involved, it is different. The federal government brings resources and power and a level of activity which is very, very significant."[18]

Laws such as the Matthew Shepard Act do not violate state and local authority. Rather, the measures would allow the federal government to bring necessary added resources and money to help in the prosecution of difficult cases. The federal government has a long history of passing remedial legislation that protects disadvantaged individuals. The Civil Rights Act of 1964, the Voting Rights Act of 1965, and the Fair Housing Act of 1968 are just three examples from recent history.

Congress has broad powers under Article 1, Section 8, Clause 3 of the Constitution, known popularly as the "Commerce Clause." This means that before the federal government can become involved, it has to be shown that the hate crime in question had an effect on interstate commerce. If an offender committed a crime by kidnapping a gay person and traveling across state lines, it would be clear that there has been sufficient interstate commerce to trigger federal law enforcement. As the

Matthew Shepard Act identifies, many hate crimes perpetrated against gay and lesbians will involve interstate travel, weapons that have traveled in interstate commerce, or will otherwise effect commerce sufficiently to allow the federal government sufficient jurisdiction to provide much-needed help in eradicating these most harmful of crimes.

Summary

Many state laws do prohibit hate crimes based on sexual orientation or gender identity. While this is good, the federal government needs to become more involved with the issue of hate crimes perpetrated against homosexuals. The federal government can bring resources and law enforcement training that cash-strapped local law enforcement officials simply cannot. Additionally, if the federal government becomes more involved, it sends a much more powerful message to society that such crimes will not be tolerated.

Homosexuals are members of a disadvantaged group who are often victims of hate crimes. Proposals to expand federal authority will not threaten religious expression and do not violate constitutional concerns. The proposed legislation does not infringe on First Amendment free-expression principles and the federal government is not overstepping its authority because the proposed legislation is carefully calibrated to ensure that Congress is acting pursuant to the Commerce Clause.

Federal Hate-Crime Laws Should Not Be Expanded to Cover Sexual Orientation

In 2003, a Swedish Pentecostal pastor named Ake Green delivered a sermon in which he preached against homosexuality. He told his congregation that homosexuals "were a deep cancer tumor on all of society." While many may object to Green's statements, the fact is that they were his sincere religious beliefs. Authorities arrested Green and charged him with violating a hate-crimes law because of these statements he made in the confines of his church. He was sentenced to 30 days in jail.[1] "I am not a criminal," Green said. "I don't feel like a criminal, but this new law makes us preachers 'as criminals' if we speak up."[2] Although appeals courts in Sweden voided his conviction, many people are fearful of expressing any opposition to homosexuality for fear of overbroad hate-crime laws that punish not only harmful conduct but protected speech.

Similar incidents have occurred in the United States of America. In 2004, four members of a conservative Christian group called Repent America were arrested in Philadelphia for picketing a gay-pride festival. Prosecutors claimed that the Christian protesters were trying to incite the crowd against the parade. These Christians, however, were not inciting a riot. Rather, they were singing religious hymns and carrying signs that opposed homosexuality. In February 2005, a city judge dismissed the charges against the protesters, writing: "We cannot stifle speech because we don't want to hear it, or we don't want to hear it now."[3]

Hate-crime laws on sexual orientation stifle religious expression.

The Ake Green and Repent America examples mentioned above show the real danger of hate-crime legislation designed to protect those allegedly victimized because of their sexual orientation.

QUOTABLE

John W. Whitehead

Finally, and most concerning of all, the Matthew Shepard Act has the potential to further suppress free speech, especially among religious individuals who disagree with homosexuality. Whether or not the law includes a provision exempting free speech, there have already been instances at home and abroad where peaceful religious expression has resulted in hate crime prosecutions. For example, Christians have been prosecuted under a state hate crime law for "singing hymns" and peacefully "carrying signs" while attending a homosexual fair in Pennsylvania. Because the signs challenged the morality of homosexuality, these Christians were charged with three felonies and five misdemeanors and faced 47 years in prison for attempting to preach at a homosexual street fair. Indeed, a state judge determined that the prosecutions could go forward. His rationale was that the Christians' speech constituted so-called "fighting words." The decision was eventually overturned.

Source: John W. Whitehead, "Criminalizing Your Thoughts," The Rutherford Institute, October 10, 2007. http://www.rutherford.org/articles_db/commentary.asp?record_id=499.

Such hate crimes are, according to Brad W. Dacus, "used as a justification for all manner of restrictions, particularly against people of faith who raise religious objections to behavior they consider immoral."[4]

In Canada, Hugh Owen purchased a newspaper ad that cited numerous biblical verses that criticized homosexuality. In 2001,

Statement from Congress: "Dissenting Views" from House Judiciary Committee Report

Ultimately, a pastor's sermon concerning religious beliefs and teachings could be considered to cause violence and will be punished or at least investigated. Once the legal framework is in place, political pressure will be placed on prosecutors to investigate pastors or other religious leaders who quote the Bible or express their long-held beliefs on the morality and appropriateness of certain behaviors. Religious teachings and common beliefs will fall under government scrutiny, chilling every American's right to worship in the manner they choose and to express their religious beliefs.

Hate crime laws could be used to target social conservatives and traditional morality. Hate crime laws have already been used to suppress speech disfavored by cultural elites—indeed this may be their principal effect. Of the 9,430 "hate crimes" recorded by the FBI by far the largest group was labeled "intimidation." The "intimidation" category does not even exist for ordinary crimes. This vague concept is already being abused by some local governments, which target speech in favor of traditional morality as "hate speech." In New York, a pastor who had rented billboards and posted biblical quotations on sexual morality had them taken down by city officials, who cited hate-crimes principles as justification. In San Francisco, the city council enacted a resolution urging local broadcast media not to run advertisements by a pro-family group, and recently passed a resolution condemning the Catholic Church because of its "hateful" views. No viewpoint should be suppressed simply because someone disagrees with it.

Source: House Committee on the Judiciary, *Local Law Enforcement Hate Crimes Prevention Act of 2007: Hearings on H.R. 1592,* 110th Cong., 1st sess., 2007, p. 41. http://frwebgate.access. gpo.gov/cgibin/getdoc.cgi?dbname=110_cong_reports&docid=f:hr113.pdf.

a trial court in his country convicted him of violating a hate-crimes law and fined him $4,500.[5] While he prevailed on appeal, the chilling effect on religious expression is palpable.

In 2000, a Kenyan-born Christian pastor named Kristopher Okwedy purchased ads on billboards in Staten Island, New York, that quoted various Bible translations of Leviticus 18:22, which reads: "Thou shalt not lie with mankind as with womankind: it is an abomination." Government officials did not charge him with a crime but they put pressure on the sign owner to remove the messages. A local official called the billboards "unnecessarily confrontational and offensive."[6] For the expression of his religious beliefs and quotation of scripture, Okwedy endured a series of threatening phone calls, racial slurs, and government opposition.[7] "It's a freedom-of-speech issue," Okwedy said. "It's not an attack on anybody. I want to be able to speak what I want, when I want. To restrict what people say in this country would compromise liberty."[8]

Even if there are no criminal charges, religious expression against the gay and lesbian movement can subject one to government investigation or opposition. In Redlands, California, a pastor faced opposition from a local human relations commission after disseminating anti-gay signs. A government commissioner told a newspaper: "No one should dictate to another person how they should live. This is not a chosen lifestyle."[9]

Hate-crime laws should not offer special protection to gays and lesbians.

Many people who do not fall into a specific group also face discrimination and hate yet do not receive special status under the law. The Matthew Shepard Act—the proposed federal law that would expand hate-crime coverage to gays and lesbians—is an example of Congress attempting to placate special-interest groups and intruding into local and state matters. "For instance, the Shepard Act singles homosexuals out for expanded protection from hate crimes yet fails to address the thousands of crimes that occur each year against people who, while not gay, just don't 'fit in,'" says civil liberties expert John W. Whitehead.[10]

Battling hate crimes should be a state and local—not a federal—issue.

One of the most important concepts in American constitutional law is federalism, a concept that deals with the allocation of power between the federal and state governments. The U.S. Supreme Court has invalidated federal laws on federalism grounds several times since 1995, reasoning that Congress essentially was stepping into areas that are state and local problems. For example, in *United States v. Lopez* (1995), the U.S. Supreme Court struck down a federal gun-control law because Congress did not have sufficient authority under the Commerce Clause. "The possession of a gun in a local school zone is in no sense an

---

QUOTABLE

U.S. Representative Louie Gohmert

This hate crimes bill says to the world that sexual orientation—and not just gender but gender identity, whatever that vague definition means—are in the same category as those persons who have suffered for the color of their skin or their religion. It says to the world that in the priorities of the majority of the United States Congress, a transvestite with gender identity issues will now be more important to protect than a heterosexual, than college or school students, or even senior citizens and widows with no gender identity issues.

Whatever happened to the idea that we were all created equal and that we all matter equally in God's eyes? We all deserve equal protection....

So the message of the hate crime legislation today is apparently this: If you are going to shoot, brutalize or hurt someone, the majority in Congress begs you not to hate us while you are shooting or brutalizing us. Please make it a random, senseless act of violence, and that does not make sense.

Source: Statement of Rep. Louie Gohmert, House Judiciary Subcommittee Hearing on H.R. 1592, *The Local Law Enforcement Hate Crimes Prevention Act of 2007*, April 17, 2007, at p. 3–4 http://judiciary.house.gov/hearings/printers/110th/34756.PDF

economic activity that might, through repetition elsewhere, substantially affect any sort of interstate commerce," Chief Justice William Rehnquist wrote for the court.[11]

In 2000, in *U.S. v. Morrison*, the U.S. Supreme Court struck down a federal law called the Violence Against Women Act that criminalized much gender-motivated violence.[12] The Court wrote that "gender-motivated crimes of violence are not, in any sense of the phrase, economic activity"[13] and that "the regulation and punishment of intrastate violence that is not directed at the instrumentalities, channels, or goods involved in interstate commerce has always been the province of the States."[14] In these decisions, a majority of the Court was concerned about federalizing crime—turning local and state crimes into federal crimes.

Summary

Many in the gay and lesbian community have trouble accepting that there have been sincere religious objections to the gay lifestyle throughout history. As John Eldsmore, senior staff attorney with the Alabama Supreme Court, wrote in 2007: "Homosexual conduct, which virtually every civilization at all times in history has condemned as immoral, harmful, and aberrant, is now lauded as an acceptable lifestyle; and a defense of traditional Biblical morality is condemned as the most vile sin of all—intolerance."[15] Unfortunately, some preachers and others who engage in sincere religious speech that opposes homosexuality have faced discrimination themselves.

There is no need for the federal government to pass a law such as the Matthew Shepard Act, which would grant special protection to a minority group in violation of the judicial concept of equal protection. Such an act would also be a violation of the Constitution's Commerce Clause; therefore, it should be left to state and local lawmakers to include "sexual orientation" in their individual local ordinances.

The Future

M uch of this book has focused on hate-crime policy and legal issues in the United States. It should be noted, however, that the issue of hate crimes is a global one. Racism, xenophobia, homophobia, and similar prejudices run rampant in various parts of the globe. Hate crimes, therefore, can occur anywhere. According to Human Rights First, "European and North American governments are failing to keep pace with a wave of violent hate crime that continues to rise across the region."[1] Given the prevalence of bias-motivated crime in the world, the organization calls for the strengthening of all types of bias-motivated criminal laws.[2] Among its 10 recommendations for world leaders was to enact laws that specifically address and punish hate crimes: "Recognizing the particular harm caused by violent hate crimes, governments should enact laws that establish specific offenses or provide enhanced penalties for

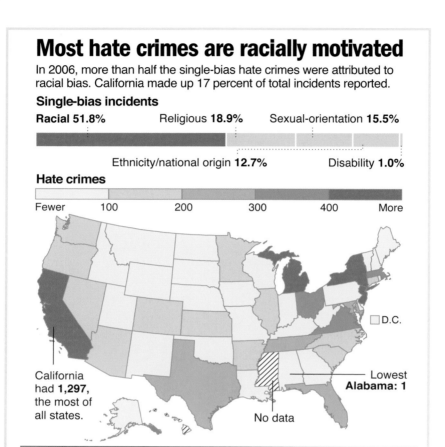

Most hate crimes are racially motivated

In 2006, more than half the single-bias hate crimes were attributed to racial bias. California made up 17 percent of total incidents reported.

Single-bias incidents

Racial 51.8%   Religious **18.9%**   Sexual-orientation **15.5%**

Ethnicity/national origin **12.7%**   Disability **1.0%**

Hate crimes

Fewer   100   200   300   400   More

California had **1,297**, the most of all states.

No data

Lowest
Alabama: 1

☐ D.C.

SOURCE: Department of Justice   AP

The graphic above shows the percentage of single-bias hate crimes by type and hate crime incidents by state in 2006.

violent crimes committed because of the victim's race, religion, ethnicity, sexual orientation, gender, gender identity, mental and physical disabilities, or other similar status."[3]

A vigorous debate over hate crimes continues, as both houses of Congress have not passed the Matthew Shepard bill as of this writing. The question of whether the federal government should become more involved in the issue of hate crimes has been a consistently controversial topic for nearly 20 years. The topic even became an issue during the 2008 presidential campaign, as Senator Barack Obama, who ultimately won the election, said that as president, he would sign the Shepard bill if it were approved by Congress.[4] On the campaign trail, Obama often emphasized that his opponent, Senator John McCain, did not have the same level of support for expanding hate-crimes coverage.

Some contend that the federal government should not be in the business of regulating crimes that are essentially are local problems. They note that most states have passed hate-crimes laws and there is no need for federalizing the issue. For example, an editorial in the *National Review* notes that "there is no evidence that local law enforcement has a special need for federal resources to help it combat hate crimes."[5] Opponents of additional federal hate-crime legislation insist that hate-crime laws violate fundamental equal-protection principles by treating some victims as more special than others. For example, the newspaper the *Oklahoman* writes that "hate crime laws discount some victims and elevate the status of others."[6]

Should State and Federal Hate-Crime Laws Protect the Homeless?

Another emerging issue is whether hate-crime statutes should be expanded to cover crime against the homeless. Tragically, the homeless are often victims of cruel and violent attacks. A particularly gruesome example of this occurred in October 2008, when John Robert McGraham was doused with gasoline and set afire for no apparent reason other than that he was homeless.[7] The National Coalition for the Homeless and other groups are pushing for greater public awareness of the violence that homeless people often face. Hate crimes against the homeless have escalated dramatically in recent years. There was a 300 percent increase in reported hate crimes against the homeless from 2002 to 2006.[8] "The homeless are at an astronomical risk of attack compared to other people," said Brian Levin, director of the

Center for the Study of Hate and Extremism, in the Southern Poverty Law Center's Intelligence Report, which monitors hate-crime issues worldwide.[9]

U.S. Representative Eddie Bernice Johnson of Texas has introduced two bills in Congress that would amend the Hate Crime Statistics Act of 1990 and the Violent Crime Control and Law Enforcement Act of 1994 to include the homeless. These are the Hate Crimes Against the Homeless Enforcement Act of 2007 and the Hate Crimes Against the Homeless Statistics Act of 2007.[10] "We want to send a message that homeless people are just as valuable as anyone else's life," said Maria Foscarinis.[11]

Another issue pertains to the continued volatility of the immigration issue and backlash against immigrants. The Intelligence Project of the Southern Poverty Law Center has identified nearly 150 "nativist extremist" groups that through their rhetoric or action have grown more extreme on this divisive political issue. Some fear that this could produce a greater number of hate crimes committed against people because of their national origin or ethnicity.[12]

Proposed Hate-Crime Law Protecting the Homeless

The Hate Crimes Against the Homeless Enforcement Act

The Violent Crime Control and Law Enforcement Act of 1994 (28 U.S.C. 994) is amended to read as follows:

(a) Definitions- In this section:

(1) HATE CRIME—The term "hate crime" means a crime in which the defendant intentionally selects a victim, or in the case of a property crime, the property that is the object of the crime, because of the actual or perceived race, color, religion, national origin, ethnicity, gender, disability, sexual orientation, or homeless status of any person.

Source: H.R. 2217, 110th Cong. 1st sess. (May 8, 2007).

Hate-crime legislation in various states is also contentious. A few states, such as Wyoming, where Matthew Shepard was viciously murdered, still have not enacted any hate-crime laws. Measures have been introduced in the Indiana Legislature virtually every year since 1999 but no bill has passed.[13]

Should Hate Speech on the Internet Be Restricted?

Finally, there is the question of regulating hate speech on the Internet. Numerous hate groups have flocked to the Web to use its capabilities to spread their message, recruit members, and, potentially, to commit more hate crimes. Given the increase in hate crimes and an increase in the ability of certain hate groups to recruit members on the Internet, the issue of whether online hate speech should receive First Amendment protection has entered public consciousness.[14] One legal commentator explains: "Clearly, the public and legislators are seeking broader and tougher laws against hate crimes. It seems likely to many people outside the courts that certain forms of hate messages do precede violent hate crimes."[15]

The Southern Poverty Law Center explains: "Video-sharing may be a particularly effective way for extremist groups, which have long sought ways to find new recruits, to connect with young people."[16] The number of extremist Web sites continues to proliferate on the Internet. The Southern Poverty Law Center identified nearly 600 U.S.-based hate sites that are active on the World Wide Web.[17] Mark Potok, editor of the *Intelligence Report*, writes that "the number of hate groups has shot up 40% in six years."[18]

What About Extremely Violent Acts Not Included in Hate-Crime Law?

A major complaint against hate crime legislation is that it doesn't treat crime equally. A related criticism is that certain awful acts—perhaps worse than individual crimes that many call hate-crimes—are not considered hate crimes. For example, when Eric Harris and Dylan Klebold opened fire on their fellow students at Columbine High School in Littleton, Colorado, the crime they committed was not officially considered a hate crime. Neither was Seung Hui Cho's murder of more than 30 of his fellow students at Virginia Tech University. Many believe that these shooting rampages are more hateful than traditional hate crimes. Supporters of hate crime legislation may argue that perhaps acts of terror should be prosecuted as hate crimes. Others contend that the disparity shows that the hate-crime concept is flawed to the core from an equal-protection perspective.

Summary

There are no easy answers to the difficult policy and legal questions raised in the hate crime debate. One thing is certain—the debate over hate crimes is far from over and will likely continue far into the twenty-first century (and possibly beyond).

Beginning Legal Research

The goals of each book in the POINT/COUNTERPOINT series are not only to give the reader a basic introduction to a controversial issue affecting society, but also to encourage the reader to explore the issue more fully. This Appendix is meant to serve as a guide to the reader in researching the current state of the law as well as exploring some of the public policy arguments as to why existing laws should be changed or new laws are needed.

Although some sources of law can be found primarily in law libraries, legal research has become much faster and more accessible with the advent of the Internet. This Appendix discusses some of the best starting points for free access to laws and court decisions, but surfing the Web will uncover endless additional sources of information. Before you can research the law, however, you must have a basic understanding of the American legal system.

The most important source of law in the United States is the Constitution. Originally enacted in 1787, the Constitution outlines the structure of our federal government, as well as setting limits on the types of laws that the federal government and state governments can enact. Through the centuries, a number of amendments have added to or changed the Constitution, most notably the first 10 amendments, which collectively are known as the "Bill of Rights" and which guarantee important civil liberties.

Reading the plain text of the Constitution provides little information. For example, the Constitution prohibits "unreasonable searches and seizures" by the police. To understand concepts in the Constitution, it is necessary to look to the decisions of the U.S. Supreme Court, which has the ultimate authority in interpreting the meaning of the Constitution. For example, the U.S. Supreme Court's 2001 decision in *Kyllo v. United States* held that scanning the outside of a person's house using a heat sensor to determine whether the person is growing marijuana is an unreasonable search—if it is done without first getting a search warrant from a judge. Each state also has its own constitution and a supreme court that is the ultimate authority on its meaning.

Also important are the written laws, or "statutes," passed by the U.S. Congress and the individual state legislatures. As with constitutional provisions, the U.S. Supreme Court and the state supreme courts are the ultimate authorities in interpreting the meaning of federal and state laws, respectively. However, the U.S. Supreme Court might find that a state law violates the U.S. Constitution, and a state supreme court might find that a state law violates either the state or U.S. Constitution.

Not every controversy reaches either the U.S. Supreme Court or the state supreme courts, however. Therefore, the decisions of other courts are also important. Trial courts hear evidence from both sides and make a decision, while appeals courts review the decisions made by trial courts. Sometimes rulings from appeals courts are appealed further to the U.S. Supreme Court or the state supreme courts.

Lawyers and courts refer to statutes and court decisions through a formal system of citations. Use of these citations reveals which court made the decision or which legislature passed the statute, and allows one to quickly locate the statute or court case online or in a law library. For example, the Supreme Court case *Brown v. Board of Education* has the legal citation 347 U.S. 483 (1954). At a law library, this 1954 decision can be found on page 483 of volume 347 of the U.S. Reports, which are the official collection of the Supreme Court's decisions. On the following page, you will find samples of all the major kinds of legal citation.

Finding sources of legal information on the Internet is relatively simple thanks to "portal" sites such as findlaw.com and lexisone.com, which allow the user to access a variety of constitutions, statutes, court opinions, law review articles, news articles, and other useful sources of information. For example, findlaw.com offers access to all Supreme Court decisions since 1893. Other useful sources of information include gpo.gov, which contains a complete copy of the U.S. Code, and thomas.loc.gov, which offers access to bills pending before Congress, as well as recently passed laws. Of course, the Internet changes every second of every day, so it is best to do some independent searching.

Of course, many people still do their research at law libraries, some of which are open to the public. For example, some state governments and universities offer the public access to their law collections. Law librarians can be of great assistance, as even experienced attorneys need help with legal research from time to time.

Common Citation Forms

Source of Law	Sample Citation	Notes
U.S. Supreme Court	*Employment Division v. Smith*, 485 U.S. 660 (1988)	The U.S. Reports is the official record of Supreme Court decisions. There is also an unofficial Supreme Court ("S. Ct.") reporter.
U.S. Court of Appeals	*United States v. Lambert*, 695 F.2d 536 (11th Cir.1983)	Appellate cases appear in the Federal Reporter, designated by "F." The 11th Circuit has jurisdiction in Alabama, Florida, and Georgia.
U.S. District Court	*Carillon Importers, Ltd. v. Frank Pesce Group, Inc.*, 913 F.Supp. 1559 (S.D.Fla.1996)	Federal trial-level decisions are reported in the Federal Supplement ("F. Supp."). Some states have multiple federal districts; this case originated in the Southern District of Florida.
U.S. Code	Thomas Jefferson Commemoration Commission Act, 36 U.S.C., §149 (2002)	Sometimes the popular names of legislation—names with which the public may be familiar—are included with the U.S. Code citation.
State Supreme Court	*Sterling v. Cupp*, 290 Ore. 611, 614, 625 P.2d 123, 126 (1981)	The Oregon Supreme Court decision is reported in both the state's reporter and the Pacific regional reporter.
State Statute	Pennsylvania Abortion Control Act of 1982, 18 Pa. Cons. Stat. 3203-3220 (1990)	States use many different citation formats for their statutes.

Cases

Brandenburg v. Ohio, 395 U.S. 444 (1969)

The U.S. Supreme Court ruled that a local Ku Klux Klan leader's racist and anti-Semitic remarks were protected under the First Amendment because it could not be shown that such remarks would incite imminent lawless action. The Brandenburg decision establishes that hate speech (without hateful criminal conduct) is often protected under First Amendment jurisprudence.

Skokie v. Nationalist Socialist Party, 373 N.E.2d 21 (Ill. 1978)

The Illinois Supreme Court protected the First Amendment rights of Nazi sympathizers to display swastikas during their march through a largely Jewish town. The case demonstrates the principle that the First Amendment protects a great deal of unpopular speech.

R.A.V. v. City of St. Paul, 505 U.S. 377 (1992)

The U.S. Supreme Court struck down a St. Paul, Minnesota, ordinance that prohibited cross-burnings and other symbolic speech done to "arouse anger or resentment" on the basis of race, sex, and other protected categories. The U.S. Supreme Court ruled that the law amounted to viewpoint discrimination under the First Amendment because it selectively criminalized certain types of expression based on the viewpoints of the offenders. Generally, *R.A.V.* stands for the proposition that hate speech is generally protected by the First Amendment.

Wisconsin v. Mitchell, 508 U.S. 476 (1993)

The U.S. Supreme Court upheld a Wisconsin hate-crime law that provided enhanced penalties for those who committed hate crimes. The defendant, Todd Mitchell, had his sentence for aggravated assault increased because he had selected his victim based on race. Mitchell, who prevailed before the Wisconsin Supreme Court, contended that the penalty-enhancement law violated the First Amendment. The U.S. Supreme Court unanimously rejected that claim, making a distinction between protected speech and unprotected conduct.

State v. McKnight, 511 N.W.2d 389 (Iowa 1994)

The Iowa Supreme Court upheld a state penalty-enhancement law from challenge by a defendant who selected his victim based on race. The Iowa court relied heavily on the rationale of *Wisconsin v. Mitchell* to reach its decision.

Virginia v. Black, 538 U.S. 343 (2003)

The U.S. Supreme Court ruled that the state of Virginia could criminalize cross-burnings that were done with "an intent to intimidate" others. The Court reasoned that many cross burnings—given their history as methods of intimidation—qualify as true threats. Under First Amendment law, true threats are not protected speech. The Court, however, struck down another provision of the Virginia cross-burning law that created a presumption that any cross burning was a true threat.

Botts v. State, 604 S.E.2d 512 (Ga. 2004)

The Georgia Supreme Court struck down a state hate-crime law that provided for enhanced penalties. The Georgia high court focused on the vague and overbroad language of the statute that allowed increased penalties anytime a defendant acted with "bias or prejudice." The court expressed grave concern that this law would not put people on notice when their conduct was criminal.

Terms and Concepts

Bias
Commerce Clause
Double jeopardy
Equal protection
Ethnic intimidation laws
Federalism
Fifth Amendment
First Amendment
Hate speech
Impartial jury
Incitement to imminent lawless action
Penalty-enhancement law
Sixth Amendment
"Slippery slope"
True threat

INTRODUCTION: What are Hate Crimes? An Overview of Their Development

1 David Ritcheson of Harris County, Texas, testifying on April 17, 2007, before the U.S. House Judiciary subcommittee, *Local Law Enforcement Hate Crimes Act of 2007 (H.R. 1562)*, at p. 67. Available online. URL: http://judiciary.house.gov/hearings/printers/110th/34756.pdf.

2 House Committee on the Judiciary, *Local Law Enforcement Hate Crimes Prevention Act of 2007: Hearings on H.R. 1592*, 110th Cong., 1st sess., 2007, 6.

3 National Criminal Justice Association and Bureau of Justice Assistance, "A Policymaker's Guide to Hate Crimes," March 1997. Available online. URL: http://www.ncjrs.gov/pdffiles1/bja/162304.pdf.

4 Jack McDevitt, testifying on April 17, 2007, before the U.S. House Subcommittee on Crime, Terrorism and Homeland Security on the *Local Law Enforcement Hate Crime Prevention Act*, Available online. URL: http://judiciary.house.gov/hearings/printers/110th/34756.pdf.

5 18 U.S. Code § 245.

6 Scott Bronstein, "Laws to Curb Bias Attacks Weighed," *New York Times*, March 2, 1987.

7 James B. Jacobs and Kimberly Potter. *Hate Crimes: Criminal Law & Identity Politics*. New York: Oxford University Press, 1998.

8 18 U.S. Code §247.

9 13 V.S.A. § 1455

10 Edward I. Koch, "Toward One Nation, Indivisible," *New York Times*, June 25, 1987.

11 Representative Sheila Jackson Lee of Texas, speaking for the *Local Law Enforcement Hate Crimes Prevention Act of 2007*, on April 17, 2007, to the House Subcommittee on Crime, Terrorism and Homeland Security, p. 12.

12 Timothy W. Lynch, speaking against the *Local Law Enforcement Hate Crimes Prevention Act of 2007*, on April 17, 2007, to the House Subcommittee on Crime, Terrorism and Homeland Security, p. 33.

13 Nat Hentoff, "Prosecuting Hate Crimes," First Amendment Center Online, June 25, 2007. Available online. URL: http://www.firstamendmentcenter.org/commentary.aspx?id=18714.

POINT: Penalty-Enhancement Laws for Hate Crimes Are Constitutional, Effective, and Necessary to Combat and Deter Hate Crimes

1 *Wisconsin v. Mitchell*, 508 U.S. 476, 480 (1993).

2 Ibid., 482.

3 Anti-Defamation League, People for the American Way, et al., brief of amici curiae in support of petitioner in *Wisconsin v. Mitchell*, p. 11.

4 Ibid.

5 Ibid., p. 5.

6 Jack McDevitt, testifying on the *Local Law Enforcement Hate Crimes Prevention Act of 2007* on April 17, 2007, to the House Judiciary subcommittee. Available online. URL: http://judiciary.house.gov/hearings/printers/110th/34756.pdf.

7 Anti-Defamation League, et al., brief of *amici curiae*, p. 6.

8 Ibid., p. 12.

9 Ibid., pp. 10–11.

10 Ibid., p. 14.

11 *Wisconsin v. Mitchell*, 508 U.S., pp. 487–488.

12 *State v. McKnight*, 511 N.W.2d 389, 395 (Iowa 1994).

13 Anti-Defamation League, et al., brief of amici curiae, p. 15.

14 Lauren Levin and Michael Sheetz, "Myths about Hate Crimes Must Be Separated from Facts of The Cases," *Jewish Advocate*, November 12, 1998, p. 12.

15 Mark L. Briskman, "Everyone Condemns Brutal Acts of Bigotry, But Is a Hate-crime Law the Right Response? YES: These Atrocities Victimize Entire Groups," *Dallas Morning News*, April 1, 2001.

16 White House news release, "President Bush Signs Identity Theft Penalty Enhancement Act," July 15, 2004. Available online. URL: http://www.whitehouse.gov/news/releases/2004/07/20040715–3.html.

17 *In re: Joshua M.*, 13 Cal. App. 4th 1734, 1751 (1993).

18 *People v. MacKenzie*, 34 Cal. App. 4th 1256, 1272 (1995).

COUNTERPOINT: Penalty-Enhancement Laws Violate the Constitution and Further Divide Society

1 Susan B. Gelman and Frederick M. Lawrence, "Agreeing to Agree: A Proponent and Opponent of Hate Crime Laws Reach for Common Ground," 41 *Harvard Journal on Legislation* 421, 426 (2004).

2 *Wisconsin v. Mitchell*, 485 N.W.2d 807, 812 (Wisc. 1992).

3 Ibid., p. 817.

4 *Botts v. State*, 604 S.E.2d 512, 514–515 (Ga. 2004).

5 Joshua S. Geller, "A Dangerous Mix: Mandatory Sentence Enhancements and the Use of Motive," Fordham Urban Law Journal 32 (2005), p. 623, 645–646.

6 *Apprendi v. New Jersey*, 530 U.S. 466 (2000).

7 Gregory R. Nearpass, "The Overlooked Constitutional Objection and Practical Concerns of Penalty-Enhancement Provisions of Hate Crime Legislation," *Albany Law Review* 66 (2003), p. 547, 562.

8 Ibid., pp. 562–563.

9 Douglas Lee, "Criminalizing Hate Shackles Everyone's Rights," First Amendment Center Online, October 30, 1998. URL: http://www.freedomforum.org/templates/document.asp?documentID=11062.

10 Timothy Lynch, testifying in opposition to the *Local Law Enforcement Hate Crimes Prevention Act of 2007* on April 17, 2007, before the House Subcommittee on Crime, Terrorism and Homeland Security, p. 36.

11 Susan B. Gellman, "Sticks and Stones Can Put You in Jail, But Can Words Increase Your Sentence? Constitutional and Policy Dilemmas of Ethnic Intimidation Laws," *UCLA Law Review* 39 (1991), p. 333, 385.

12 Karen Franklin, "Good Intentions: The Enforcement of Hate Crime Penalty-Enhancement Statutes," in *Crimes of Hate: Selected Readings*, Phyllis B. Grestenfeld and Diana R. Grant, eds. Thousand Oaks, CA: Sage Publications, 2004: 79–92.

13 Ibid., p. 82.

14 Quoted in Ryan Myers, "Jasper: The Road Back," *Beaumont Enterprise*, June 6, 2008.

15 Ibid.

16 Karen Franklin, "Good Intentions: The Enforcement of Hate Crime Penalty-Enhancement Statutes," p. 87.

17 Edward Rothstein, "Hate Crimes: What is Gained When Forbidden Acts Become Forbidden Beliefs?" *New York Times*, September 19, 2005.

POINT: The Display of a Noose is a Hate Crime and Noose-Display Laws are Constitutional

1 Associated Press, "Rash of Noose Incidents Reported Across the Country In Wake of Jena Six Case," *Mobile Register*, October 11, 2007.

2 Chris Bonnette, "Munsen Gets Four Months in Noose Case," *Daily Town Talk* (Alexandria, LA), August 16, 2008.

3 Equal Employment Opportunity Commission news release, "Henredon Furniture Industries to Pay $465,000 for Racial Harassment, Hangman's Nooses," January 24, 2008. Available online. URL: http://www.eeoc.gov/press/1–24–08.html.

4 Testimony of John Hendrickson, EEOC regional attorney, Transcript of EEOC meeting, February 28, 2007. Available online. URL: http://www.eeoc.gov/abouteeoc/meetings/2–28–07/transcript.html.

5 National Association for the Advancement of Colored People, "State of Emergency: Stemming the Tide of Injustice Against African-Americans," November 2007, p. 6. Available online. URL: http://www.naacp.org/pdfs/NAACP-state-of-emergency.pdf.

6 SR 396, 110th Cong., 1st Session, December 14, 2007. Available online. URL: http://thomas.loc.gov.

7 Connecticut Public Act No. 08–49. Available online. URL: http://www.cga.ct.gov/2008/ACT/PA/2008PA-00049-R00SB-00604-PA.htm.

8 State of Connecticut news release, "Governor Rell Signs New Law Banning Use of Nooses to Threaten or Intimidate," May 11, 2008. Available online. URL:

http://www.ct.gov/GovernorRell/cwp/view.asp?A=3293&Q=414922.

9 State of New York news release, "Governor Paterson Signs Legislation to Outlaw Display of a Noose as a Means of Intimidation," May 15, 2008. Available online. URL: http://www.state.ny.us/governor/press/press_0515082.html.

10 Louisiana House Bill No. 726. Available online. URL: http://www.legis.state.la.us/billdata/streamdocument.asp?did=498903.

11 *Virginia v. Black*, 538 U.S. 343 (2003).

12 Ibid., p. 363.

13 Quoted in David L. Hudson Jr., "States move to add nooses to list of outlawed symbols," First Amendment Center Online, June 28, 2008. Available online. URL: http://www.firstamendmentcenter.org/analysis.aspx?id=20234.

COUNTERPOINT: Banning the Display of Nooses Is Unnecessary and Unconstitutional

1 *Texas v. Johnson*, 491 U.S. 397, 407 (1989).

2 *Skokie v. Nationalist Socialist Party*, 373 N.E.2d 21 (Ill. 1978).

3 *Hustler v. Falwell*, 485 U.S. 46 (1988).

4 *Brandenburg v. Ohio*, 395 U.S. 444 (1969).

5 Mike Riggs, "Noose Laws Hang Free Speech," *Reason*, July 22, 2008. Available online. URL: http://www.reason.com/blog/show/127685.html.

6 Carol Swain, "Why Black Americans Shouldn't Be Focused on Hanging Nooses," *Sun* (Baltimore), December 5, 2007.

7 *Police Dept. of City of Chicago v. Mosley*, 408 U.S. 92, 96 (1972).

8 *Tinker v. Des Moines Independent Community School District*, 393 U.S. 503 (1969).

9 *R.A.V. v. City of St. Paul*, 505 U.S. 377 (1992).

10 Ibid., p. 378.

11 David L. Hudson Jr., "States Move to Add Nooses to List of Outlawed Symbols," First Amendment Center Online, June 28, 2008. Available online. URL: http://www.firstamendmentcenter.org/analysis.aspx?id=20234.

12 Quoted in Ed Anderson, "Plan to prohibit noose displays runs into static; ACLU chief says bill would curb free speech," *Times-Picayune* (New Orleans), March 7, 2008.

13 "Noose bill misguided," *Advocate* (Baton Rouge, LA), June 5, 2008.

14 *Texas v. Johnson*, p. 417.

15 "Free Speech Left Hanging," *New York Post*, October 24, 2007.

POINT: The Federal Government Must Do More to Protect Victims of Hate Crimes Based on Sexual Orientation

1 Human Rights First, "2008 Hate Crime Survey: Overview." Available online. URL: http://www.humanrightsfirst.org/pdf/fd/08/fd-080924-hc08-overview-web.pdf.

2 James Brooke, "Gay Man Beaten and Left for Dead," *New York Times*, October 10, 1998.

3 Rebecca Cathcart, "Boy's Killing, Labeled a Hate Crime, Stuns a Town," *New York Times*, February 23, 2008. Available online. URL: http://www.nytimes.com/2008/02/23/us/23oxnard.html.

4 Kathleen A. Bantley, "Judicial Activism and Progressive Legislation: A Step Towards Decreasing Hate Attacks," *Albany Law Review* 71 (2008), p. 545, 546.

5 Ibid., pp. 546–547.

6 Representative Conyers of Michigan, speaking for the *Local Law Enforcement Hate Crimes Prevention Act of 2007*, on April 17, 2007, to the House Subcommittee on Crime, Terrorism and Homeland Security, at p. 4. Available online. URL: http://judiciary.house.gov/hearings/printers/110th/34756.pdf.

7 Assistant U.S. Attorney Eric Holder, Senate Judiciary Committee, "Combating Hate Crimes: Promoting a Responsive and Responsible Role for the Federal Government," May 11, 1999. Available online. URL: http://www.senate.gov/comm/judiciary/general/oldsite/51199ehh.htm.

8 Senator Specter of Pennsylvania, Senate Judiciary Committee, "Combating

Hate Crimes: Promoting a Responsive and Responsible Role for the Federal Government," Hearing on Hate Crimes, May 11, 1999.

9 Federal Bureau of Investigation, "Hate Crime Statistics 2007, Table 1—Incidents, Victims, and Known Offenders." Available online. URL: http://www.fbi.gov/ucr/hc2007/table_01.htm.

10 Federal Bureau of Investigation, "FBI Releases 2007 Hate Crimes Statistics," October 27, 2008. Available online. URL: http://www.fbi.gov/ucr/hc2007/summary.htm.

11 Bantley, "Judicial Activism and Progressive Legislation," p. 552.

12 House Committee on the Judiciary, *Local Law Enforcement Hate Crimes Prevention Act of 2007: Hearings on H.R. 1592*, 110th Cong., 1st sess., 2007, p. 97. Available online. URL: http://frwebgate.access.gpo.gov/cgi-bin/getdoc.cgi?dbname=110_cong_reports&docid=f:hr113.pdf.

13 House Committee, *Hate Crimes Prevention Act*, p. 11.

14 Ibid.

15 Ibid., p. 16.

16 Charles C. Haynes, "Would Federal Hate Crimes Law Threaten Religious Freedom," First Amendment Center Online, June 10, 2007. Available online. URL: http://www.firstamendmentcenter.org/commentary.aspx?id=18648.

17 Ibid.

18 Sen. Arlen Specter, Senate Judiciary Committee, Combating Hate Crimes: Promoting a Responsive and Responsible Role for the Federal Government," Hearing on Hate Crimes, May 11, 1999.

COUNTERPOINT: Federal Hate-Crime Laws Should Not Be Expanded More to Cover Sexual Orientation

1 "Pastor Ake Green," *Swedish Press*, May 2005, p. 13.

2 Quoted in Tim Dailey, "The Slippery Slope of Thought Crimes ('Hate Crimes') Laws," Family Research Council, May 16, 2007.

3 Associated Press, "Charges dropped against anti-gay protesters," First Amendment Center Online, February 18. 2005. Available online. URL: http://www.firstamendmentcenter.org//news.aspx?id=14851.

4 Brad W. Dacus, speaking against the *Local Law Enforcement Hate Crime Prevention Act of 2007* on April 17, 2007, before the House Judiciary Subcommittee, 110th Cong., 1st sess., at p. 76.

5 John M. Templeton Jr., "Freedom of Religious Speech: Some Preachers Believe That Homosexuality Is a Sin. What If 'Hate Speech' Laws Prosecute Them for Saying So," *Pittsburgh Post-Gazette*, June 10, 2006.

6 Frank Donnelly, "Anti-Gay Pastor Seeks Ruling by Supreme Court on Billboard," *Staten Island Advance* (New York), February 9, 2007.

7 Rod Dreher, "A Most Hateful Way to Stifle Free Speech," *New York Post*, March 12, 2000.

8 Donnelly, "Anti-gay pastor seeks ruling."

9 John Andrews, "Workshop to discuss church's anti-gay messages; Redlands Human Relations Commission sets meeting on controversy," *Press-Enterprise* (Riverside, CA), March 16, 1999.

10 John W. Whitehead, "Criminalizing Your Thoughts," The Rutherford Institute, October 10, 2007. Available online. URL: http://www.rutherford.org/articles_db/commentary.asp?record_id=499.

11 *United States v. Lopez*, 514 U.S. 549, 567 (1995).

12 *United States v. Morrison*, 529 U.S. 598 (2000).

13 Ibid., p. 613.

14 Ibid., p. 616.

15 John Eldsmore, "Is Telling Lawyer Jokes a Hate Crime?" *New American*, April 2, 2007, p. 22.

CONCLUSION: The Future

1 Human Rights First, "2008 Hate Crime Survey: Overview." Available online. URL: http://www.humanrightsfirst.org/pdf/fd/08/fd-080924-hc08-overview-web.pdf.

2 Ibid.

3 Human Rights First, "2008 Hate Crime Survey: Recommendations for Government." Available online. URL: http://

www.humanrightsfirst.org/pdf/fd/08/
fd-080924-hc08-recs-web.pdf.

4 Barack Obama 2008 campaign Web
site. http://origin.barackobama.
com/issues/civil_rights/.

5 *National Review*, "Hating Hate," May 1,
2007.

6 *Oklahoman*, "No extras; Hate crime
add-ons wrong," June 24, 2008.

7 Alison Stateman, "Violence Against the
Homeless: Is It a Hate Crime?" *Time*,
October 22, 2008. Available online.
URL: http://www.time.com/time/
printout/0,8816,1852825,00.html.

8 Brentin Mock, "Hating the Homeless:
As Attacks Rise Around the Country,
A Debate on Extending Hate Crime
Laws to Protect the Homeless Divides
Advocates," *Intelligence Report* (Summer
2007), pp. 20–25, 20.

9 Quoted in Mock, p. 24.

10 *Hate Crimes Against the Homeless
Enforcement Act of 2007*, H.R. 2217,
110th Cong. 1st sess. (May 8, 2007);
*Hate Crimes Against the Homeless Statis-
tics Act of 2007*, H.R. 2216, 110th Cong.,
1st sess. (May 8. 2007).

11 Statesman, "Violence Against the
Homeless."

12 Susy Buchanan and David Holthouse,
"Shoot, Shovel, Shut Up: As the anti-
immigration movement grows even
more vitriolic, the Intelligence Project identifies 144 'nativist, extremist'
groups," *Intelligence Report* (Spring
2007), pp. 44–47.

13 Brian M. Boyce, "Indiana without 'hate
crime' laws," *Tribune-Star* (Terre Haute,
Ind.), March 26, 2008.

14 Brett A. Barnett. *Untangling the Web
of Hate: Are Online 'Hate Sites' Deserving of First Amendment Protection?*
Youngstown, NY: Cambria Press, 2007.

15 Laura Leets, "Responses to Internet
Hate Sites: Is Speech Too Free in Cyberspace?" 6 *Communication Law & Policy*
287, 317 (2001).

16 Brentin Mock, "Sharing the Hate:
Video-sharing websites like YouTube
have become the hottest new venue
for extremist propaganda and recruit-
ment," *Intelligence Report* (Spring
2007), p. 16.

17 "Hate Websites Active in the Year
2006," *Intelligence Report* (Spring 2007),
p. 59.

18 Mark Potok, "Behind the Noose," *Intelligence Report* (Winter 2007).

Books and Articles

Abel, Jason A. "Americans Under Attack: The Need for Federal Hate Crime Legislation in Light of Post-September 11 Attacks on Arab Americans and Muslims." 12 *Asian Law Journal* 41 (2005).

Abrahamson, Shirley, Susan Craighead, and Daniel Abrahamson. "Words and Sentences: Penalty Enhancement for Hate Crimes." 16 *University of Arkansas at Little Rock Law Review.* 515 (1994).

Altschiller, Donald. *Hate Crimes.* Santa Barbara, Calif.: ABC-CLIO, 2005.

Barnett, Brett A. *Untangling the Web of Hate: Are Online "Hate Sites" Deserving of First Amendment Protection?* Youngstown, N.Y.: Cambria Press, 2007.

Boeckmann, Robert J., and Carolyn Turpin-Petrosino. "Understanding the Harm of Hate Crime." 58 *Journal of Social Issues* 207 (2002).

Cathcart, Rebecca. "Boy's Killing, Labeled a Hate Crime, Stuns a Town." *New York Times,* February 23, 2008. Available online. URL: http://www.nytimes.com/2008/02/23/us/23oxnard.html.

Davis, Rebecca. "Opportunistic Hate Crimes Targeting Symbolic Property: When Free Speech Is Not Free." 10 *Journal of Gender, Race & Justice.* 93 (2006).

DeMaske, Chris. "Modern Power and the First Amendment: Reassessing Hate Speech." 9 *Communications Law & Policy* 273 (2004).

Geller, Joshua S. "A Dangerous Mix: Mandatory Sentence Enhancements and the Use of Motive." 32 *Fordham Urban Law Journal* 623 (2005).

Gellman, Susan B. "Sticks and Stones Can Put You in Jail, But Can Words Increase Your Sentence? Constitutional and Policy Dilemmas of Ethnic Intimidation Laws." 39 *UCLA Law Review.* 333 (1991).

Gellman, Susan B., and Frederick M. Lawrence. "Agreeing to Agree: A Proponent and Opponent of Hate Crime Laws Reach for Common Ground." 41 *Harvard Journal on Legislation* 421 (2004).

Gerstenfeld, Phyllis B. *Hate Crimes: Causes, Controls and Controversies.* Thousand Oaks, Calif.: SAGE Publications, 2003.

Gerstenfeld, Phyllis B., and Diana R. Grant, eds. *Crimes of Hate: Selected Readings.* Thousand Oaks, Calif.: SAGE Publications, 2004.

Gey, Steven G. "What if *Wisconsin v. Mitchell* Had Involved Martin Luther King Jr.? The Constitutional Flaws of Hate Crime Enhancement Statutes." 65 *George Washington Law Review* 1014 (1997).

Hall, Nathan. *Hate Crime*. Portland, Ore.: Willan Publishing, 2005.

Han, Eun Hee. "Hate Crimes and Hate Speech." 7 *Georgetown Journal of Gender and Law* 679 (2006).

Haynes, Charles C. "Would federal hate-crimes law threaten religious freedom?" First Amendment Center Online, June 10, 2007. Available online. URL: http://www.firstamendmentcenter.org/commentary.aspx?id=18648.

Hentoff, Nat. "Prosecuting hate crimes." First Amendment Center Online, June 25, 2007. Available online. URL: http://www.firstamendmentcenter.org/commentary.aspx?id=18714.

Herek, Gregory M., and Kevin T. Berrill, eds. *Hate Crimes: Confronting Violence Against Lesbians and Gay Men*. Thousand Oaks, Calif.: SAGE Publications, 1991.

Hudson, David L. Jr. "States move to add nooses to list of outlawed symbols." First Amendment Center Online, June 28, 2008. Available online. URL: http://www.firstamendmentcenter.org/analysis.aspx?id=20234.

Hughes, Lawrence Bradford. "Can Anyone Be the Victim of a Hate Crime?" 23 *Dayton Law Review*. 591 (1998).

Hurd, Heidi, and Michael S. Moore. "Punishing Hatred and Prejudice." 56 *Stanford Law Review* 1081 (2004).

Iganski, Paul, ed. *The Hate Debate: Should Hate Be Punished as a Crime?* London: Profile Books, 2002.

Jacobs, James B., and Kimberly Potter. *Hate Crimes: Criminal Law & Identity Politics*. New York: Oxford University Press, 1998.

Jenness, Valerie, and Ryken Grattet. *Making Hate a Crime: From Social Movement to Law Enforcement*. Thousand Oaks, Calif.: SAGE Publications, 2004.

King, Joyce. *Hate Crime: The Story of a Dragging in Jasper, Texas*. New York: Pantheon Books, 2002.

Knechtle, John C. "When to Regulate Hate Speech." 110 *Penn State Law Review* 539 (2006).

Lawrence, Frederick M. "Commentary: Federal Bias Crime Law Symposium." 80 *Boston University Law Review* 1437 (2000).

Lawrence, Frederick M. "Resolving the Hate Crimes/Hate Speech Paradox: Punishing Bias Crimes and Protecting Racist Speech." 68 *Notre Dame Law Review* 673 (1993).

Lee, Douglas. "Criminalizing hate shackles everyone's rights." First Amendment Center Online, October 30, 1998. Available online. URL: http://www.freedomforum.org/templates/document.asp?documentID= 11062.

Leets, Laura. "Responses to Internet Hate Sites: Is Speech Too Free in Cyberspace?" 6 *Communication Law & Policy* 287 (2001).

Levin, Jack. *The Violence of Hate: Confronting Racism, Anti-Semitism, and Other Forms of Bigotry,* 2nd ed. New York: Allyn & Bacon, 2006.

Levin, Jack, and Jack McDevitt. *Hate Crimes Revisited: America's War on Those Who Are Different.* New York: Basic Books, 2002.

Levy, Daniel M. "Criminal Law: Hate Crime Laws: Cure or Placebo?" 79 *Michigan Bar Journal* 674 (June 2000).

Matsuda, Mari J. "Public Response to Racist Speech: Considering the Victim's Story." 87 *Michigan Law Review* 2320 (1989).

McCoy, Scott D. "The Homosexual-Advance Defense and Hate Crime Statutes: Their Interaction and Conflict." 22 *Cardozo Law Review.* 629 (2001).

McFarland, Jeffrey M. "Penalty Enhancement for Bigoted Beliefs." 45 *Florida Law Review.* 743 (1993).

National Association for the Advancement of Colored People. "State of Emergency: Stemming the Tide of Injustice Against African-Americans." November 2007. Available online. URL: http://www.naacp.org/pdfs/ NAACP-state-of-emergency.pdf.

Nearpass, Gregory R. "The Overlooked Constitutional Objection and Practical Concerns to Penalty-Enhancement Provisions of Hate Crime Legislation." 66 *Albany Law Review* 547 (2003).

Perry, Barbara. *In the Name of Hate: Understanding Hate Crime.* New York: Routledge, 2001.

Pfeiffer, Laura. "To Enhance or Not to Enhance: Civil Penalty Enhancement for Parents of Juvenile Hate Crime Offenders." 41 *Valparaiso University Law Review.* 1685 (2007).

Rothstein, Edward. "Hate Crimes: What is Gained When Forbidden Acts Become Forbidden Beliefs?" *New York Times*, September 19, 2005.

Scotting, Troy. "Hate Crimes and the Need for Stronger Federal Legislation." 34 *Akron Law Review* 353 (2001).

Shimamoto, Eric. "Rethinking Hate Crime in the Age of Terror." 72 *University of Missouri-Kansas City School of Law* 829 (2004).

Taslitz, Andrew. "Condemning the Racist Personality: Why the Critics of Hate Crimes Legislation Are Wrong." 40 *Boston College Law Review* 739 (1999).

U.S. Department of Justice Office of Justice Programs. "A Policymaker's Guide to Hate Crimes." March 1997. Available online. URL: http://www.ncjrs.gov/pdffiles1/bja/162304.pdf.

Wang, Lui-In, "The Transforming Power of 'Hate': Social Cognition Theory and the Harms of Bias-Related Crime." 71 *Southern California Law Review* 47 (1997).

Winer, Anthony S. "Hate Crimes, Homosexuals and the Constitution." 29 *Harvard Civil Rights and Civil Liberties Journal* 387 (1994).

Web Sites
Anti-Defamation League
http://www.adl.org
> This group fights on behalf of hate-crime victims and supports penalty-enhancement laws. This Web site is an excellent resource to track state hate-crime laws.

Center for the Study of Hate and Extremism
http://hatemonitor.csusb.edu/
> This center, located on the campus of California State University, San Bernardino, describes itself as a "nonpartisan domestic research and policy center that serves the region and nation by examining the ways that bigotry, advocacy of extreme methods, or the use of terrorism deny civil or human rights to people on the basis of race, ethnicity, religion, gender, sexual orientation, disability or other relevant status characteristics."

CivilRights.Org

http://www.civilrights.org/issues/hate/hate-crime-resources.html

This coalition of different civil-rights organization contains resources for those who want to learn more about hate crimes.

Coalition Against Hate Crimes

http://www.againsthate.pdx.edu/

This Portland, Oregon-based group tracks hate crimes in that state.

Federal Bureau of Investigation, Hate Crimes Statistics

http://www.fbi.gov/hq/cid/civilrights/hate.htm

This federal law enforcement agency has the primary responsibility for compiling hate-crime statistics and provides a wealth of information on its Web site.

Human Rights First

http://www.humanrightsfirst.org/

On its site, this group declares that it "believes that building respect for human rights and the rule of law will help ensure the dignity to which every individual is entitled and will stem tyranny, extremism, intolerance, and violence." The organization's site has excellent information about hate crimes worldwide.

Jack Levin on Violence

http://www.jacklevinonviolence.com/

This is the Web site of a leading scholar and author on hate crimes.

Matthew Shepard Foundation

http://www.matthewshepard.org/site/PageServer

This foundation seeks "to educate and enlighten others on the importance of diversity, understanding, compassion, acceptance, and respect. Everyone must participate in developing solutions to problems that are rooted in ignorance and hatred."

Southern Poverty Law Center

http://www.splcenter.org

This civil-rights group serves as a watchdog against discrimination, hatred, and intolerance in America. It publishes an informative quarterly publication titled *Intelligence Report* that tracks hate-crimes and hate-speech issues.

PICTURE CREDITS ⫸

DAVID L. HUDSON JR. is a First Amendment Scholar at the First Amendment Center at Vanderbilt University. He teaches law classes at Middle Tennessee State University, Nashville School of Law, and Vanderbilt Law School. He is the author or co-author of more than 20 books, including several in the POINT/COUNTERPOINT series.

ALAN MARZILLI, M.A., J.D., lives in Birmingham, Ala., and is a program associate with Advocates for Human Potential, Inc., a research and consulting firm based in Sudbury, Mass., and Albany, N.Y. He primarily works on developing training and educational materials for agencies of the federal government on topics such as housing, mental health policy, employment, and transportation. He has spoken on mental health issues in 30 states, the District of Columbia, and Puerto Rico; his work has included training mental health administrators, nonprofit management and staff, and people with mental illnesses and their families on a wide variety of topics, including effective advocacy, community-based mental health services, and housing. Marzilli has written several handbooks and training curricula that are used nationally and as far away as the U.S. territory of Guam. Additionally, he managed statewide and national mental health advocacy programs and worked for several public interest lobbying organizations while studying law at Georgetown University. Marzilli has written more than a dozen books, including numerous titles in the POINT/COUNTERPOINT series.